T0243997

THE

HOME
MIXOLOGIST

THE HOME MIXOLOGIST

Copyright © 2024 by Cider Mill Press Book Publishers LLC.

This is an officially licensed book by Cider Mill Press Book Publishers LLC.

All rights reserved under the Pan-American and International Copyright Conventions.

No part of this book may be reproduced in whole or in part, scanned, photocopied, recorded, distributed in any printed or electronic form, or reproduced in any manner whatsoever, or by any information storage and retrieval system now known or hereafter invented, without express written permission of the publisher, except in the case of brief quotations in critical articles and reviews.

The scanning, uploading, and distribution of this book via the internet or via any other means without permission of the publisher is illegal and punishable by law. Please support authors' rights, and do not participate in or encourage piracy of copyrighted materials.

13-Digit ISBN: 978-1-40034-069-9

10-Digit ISBN: 1-40034-069-1

This book may be ordered by mail from the publisher. Please include $5.99 for postage and handling. Please support your local bookseller first!

Books published by Cider Mill Press Book Publishers are available at special discounts for bulk purchases in the United States by corporations, institutions, and other organizations. For more information, please contact the publisher.

Cider Mill Press Book Publishers
"Where good books are ready for press"
501 Nelson Place
Nashville, Tennessee 37214
cidermillpress.com

Typography: Rig Sans, Rig Shaded, Rufina

Image Credits: Pages 8-9, 33, 37, 38, and 96 used under official license from Shutterstock. Page 10 by Redd F. on Unsplash. All other photos courtesy of Cider Mill Press.

Printed in Malaysia

24 25 26 27 28 OFF 5 4 3 2 1

First Edition

SHAKE UP YOUR COCKTAIL GAME
WITH OVER 150 EASY, ELEVATED RECIPES

THE
HOME
MIXOLOGIST

CIDER MILL
PRESS

BOOK
PUBLISHERS

❧ EDITED BY SHANE CARLEY ❧

CONTENTS

INTRODUCTION

Compared to the oldest alcoholic beverages, which some researchers claim originated around 10,000 BCE, the cocktail is a relative newcomer to the spirits world, having been around for just a few hundred years—the first written record of the word "cocktail" occurs in The Farmers Cabinet, which was published in 1803.

Why, you might be wondering, did it take so long for the cocktail to emerge?

The answer depends on who you ask, but my personal favorite theory centers around the arrival of Prohibition in America—and it boils down to the fact that most of the alcohol available to the public was, to be frank, bad. Awful. Pure swill. Bootleggers needed a metaphorical spoonful of sugar to help their medicine go down, and the cocktail proved to be a godsend.

Mixed drinks had been around for some time before the start of Prohibition, but once it arrived they became all the rage. And as drinkers gathered in speakeasies and greedily imbibed these concoctions that made the rotgut they were used to seem refreshing, a social culture started to grow up around them.

Still, serving as a tentpole of social life is a long way off from evolving into an artform. But, over the last thirty or so years, that is precisely what happened—and a quick survey of the drinks scene today reveals the power of this unlikely development. All of a sudden, you can find a clarified milk punch in a sleepy mountain town. In chain restaurants, which thrive by shooting for the dead center of the road, carefully constructed drinks featuring mezcal, amaro, and housemade herbal syrups are routine, so commonplace that we take their presence for granted, barely raise an eyebrow when we encounter them.

This book aims to celebrate this evolution from bartending to mixology. It seeks not only to celebrate the new classics that have come out of it, but to instruct, illuminate the attention to detail, imagination, and craft that have gone into it.

My previous cocktail books have focused on bringing the cocktail into the home and making it accessible—they emphasize simple recipes and everyday ingredients. And while *The Home Bartender* series has been my pride and joy, and the books that I turn to most often when cocktail hour arrives—there are occasions when one wants to see what is possible. These recipes, while still accessible, fully embrace the creative side of the drinks world and the unique and the unusual spirits that have resulted from the contemporary craft distilling boom. They eschew the mundane to highlight the wild—and sometimes wacky—creations that reveal to the home bartender what a cocktail is capable of.

That isn't to say this book is full of cocktails you could never hope to make at home. On the contrary—I've done my best to include a broad selection of drinks featuring a wide range of ingredients. Some you may be able to make with the bottles you already have on hand. Others will encourage you to search out an in-

gredient whose existence you were previously unaware of. Still more will inspire you to reach for the top shelf, rather than trawling the lower levels looking for a bargain to add to your liquor cabinet.

The purpose of this book is to provide you with a glimpse of the highest levels of cocktail creation—to learn how the world's best bartenders approach their craft. To show you that, while classic cocktails are classics for a reason, creative minds across the globe are iterating on them, making tweaks, changes, and substitutions that turn familiar flavors into something novel. To do this, they deploy saline solutions, plum liqueurs, and caraway tinctures—all of which feature in recipes here. You'll find plenty of touchstones, such as vodka, whiskey, and rum, but you'll also find aquavit, Chartreuse, and shochu. You'll find recipes that date back to the 1800s and startlingly modern concoctions. You'll find frozen cocktails, shooters, and drinks topped with luscious foam. You'll find spicy drinks, sweet drinks, and everything in between. But most importantly, you'll find drinks that are certain to expand your horizons and step up your cocktail game.

BASIC TECHNIQUES

DRY SHAKE

When a recipe asks you to "dry shake," that means to combine all of the drink's ingredients in a cocktail shaker without ice and shake. The dry shake is often used to emulsify drinks that include an egg white.

WHIP SHAKE

This involves rapidly shaking a cocktail shaker or mixing tin back and forth with both hands while keeping a tight grip on it, using a minimal amount of ice. This creates a frothy texture and adds considerably more air bubbles to the drink.

DOUBLE-STRAIN

Eager to eliminate those pesky ice shards that end up in a drink? That's where the double-strain comes in. It involves straining the drink twice—once through a regular strainer (i.e., a Hawthorne strainer) and then again through a fine-mesh strainer. This ensures that any ice shards or small pieces of fruit, herbs, or spices are caught and do not end up in the final cocktail.

CUBAN ROLL

Residing in the space between shaking and stirring (more dilution and aeration than the former and yet gentler than shaking, this method consists of pouring the ingredients and ice between two containers until they are chilled and combined.

SWIZZLE METHOD

Used to combine cocktails featuring crushed ice, the swizzle method will quickly chill and aerate the cocktail. Some bartenders believe that this method also further draws out the aromas of the drink's ingredients. To employ the swizzle method, fill the glass with crushed ice, strain the cocktail over it, and place a swizzle stick between your hands. Lower the swizzle stick into the drink, and quickly rub your palms together to rotate the stick as you move it up and down in the drink. When frost begins to form on the outside of the glass, the drink is ready.

RIMMING A GLASS

To proper rim a glass with salt, sugar, or spices, fill a small bowl with ¼ cup water and a shallow bowl with ¼ cup of whatever you are applying to the rim. Wet the rim of the glass in the water, roll the rim of the glass in the salt, sugar, or spices ensuring an even coating, and gently shake off any excess.

ESSENTIAL TOOLS

There are not many things that you need to purchase in order to start crafting cocktails, but there are some rudimentary supplies that are necessary if you want to try your hand at this game.

The following pages contain the must-haves for a basic bar setup. Keep in mind that you don't have to break the bank to start your home bar, but between glassware and bar tools, a little money will need to be spent. You can find basic bar and glassware sets on specialty sites like Cocktail Kingdom, as well as at other online retailers. As with anything, the options will fit lots of budgets. If you are tight on funds, don't be deterred by secondhand items. Soap and water come pretty cheap and you might find some real bargains on vintage gear to boot. Same goes for antique shops and yard sales. Hell, your parents might have some of the tools you need stashed away in a closet or basement. Nothing wrong with a little scavenging for a good cause.

JIGGER

A jigger is just a fancy name for the most common measuring tool in a bartender's arsenal, allowing you to quickly and easily measure "parts" or ounces. Most have a similar shape and capacity to a shot glass.

MIXING GLASS

Nothing more than a tall glass in which to stir a drink. Typically a pint glass is used, but in a pinch, you can use any glass large enough to hold the necessary ingredients along with a few ice cubes.

COCKTAIL SHAKER

A cocktail shaker is a container about the size of a pint glass, usually made from metal, with a screw top. The shaker provides a simple way to mix a cocktail, both combining the necessary ingredients, chilling them with ice, and diluting the cocktail slightly to remove the bite of the included spirits and allow their flavors to come to the fore. A basic cocktail shaker is relatively inexpensive, and you are better off purchasing this specific tool than trying to jury-rig a shaker for yourself.

The three-piece shaker, which is what you'll find in most homes, is known as the "Cobbler shaker." There are also two-piece shakers, consisting of two conical containers with flat bottoms, with one of the cones larger than the other. Known as a "Boston" or "French" shaker, these tend to be favored by professional bartenders because their "throw," the amount of space inside for the ingredients and ice to become combined, is greater than in the squatter Cobbler shaker.

HAWTHORNE STRAINER

Used in tandem with either a mixing glass or Boston shaker, the Hawthorne strainer simply strains the cocktail after it has been mixed. The strainer's spring keeps the ice cubes (in the case of a mixing glass) or broken ice chips (in the case of a Boston shaker) out of a drink. Because ice waters down a drink when it melts, the strainer is an important tool for keeping a cocktail pure.

You may also come across a Julep strainer as you start making your way into the world of mixology. This strainer, which was the predecessor to the Hawthorne, is a perforated, concave disk with holes in it. It has fallen out of common use, but is the preferred tool of some bartenders when straining a cocktail containing small pieces of herb or a large amount of pulp.

PARING KNIFE

Chances are, there's already one in your kitchen, and it is essential for crafting the lemon-twist and lime-wedge garnishes that are a crucial part of numerous cocktails.

MUDDLER

Similar to a pestle, this simple tool is used to mash ("muddle") ingredients such as fruits or herbs. Muddling fruits releases the juice within, adding a fresh characteristic to a drink, while muddling certain herbs helps activate their flavors. A simple muddler can often be found on the top end of a Cobbler shaker, though more refined muddlers are available for minimal cost.

BAR SPOON

There are plenty of fancy bar spoons, but most take the form of a spoon with a small bowl and a long, threaded shaft. Used in conjunction with a mixing glass, the purpose of the bar spoon is to quickly and easily stir any cocktail. You can use any spoon—you just may find it more difficult to navigate the ice cubes. You will also come across some recipes that call for a "bar spoon" of a certain ingredient, which is equivalent to 1 teaspoon.

BOTTLES FOR HOMEMADE BITTERS & INFUSIONS

Making your own bitters and infusing liquors with herbs and spices is a tremendous, and simple, way to lift your bartending game to another level. A large mason jar also fits the bill.

COCKTAIL GLASSES

The elegant promise of the iconic thin stem and triangular bowl has become inseparable from the very idea of a cocktail, as evidenced by its frequent inclusion on a bar's signage. It is typically utilized in cocktails that are served "up," such as the Martini.

COLLINS GLASSES

Collins glasses are tall and skinny, and most commonly used in drinks that contain ice and a carbonated element such as club soda.

ROCKS GLASSES

Also known as Old Fashioned glasses, these are meant for neat drinks and spirits on the rocks. They are between 8 and 10 ounces; double rocks glasses are typically only a couple ounces larger and used for cocktails served over ice.

COUPES

The coupe has started to replace the traditional cocktail glass as the go-to for drinks that are served up, as its sleek curves lend a drink an appealing refinement.

SHOT GLASSES

There is no standard size for a shot glass, but most land between 1¼ and 1½ ounces. They can be used to measure parts for a cocktail or to serve alcohol, both straight up and mixed.

WINEGLASSES & CHAMPAGNE FLUTES

Both are sophisticated and celebratory. Wineglasses are wonderful for aromatic cocktails, while the thin bowl and delicate stem of a Champagne flute is a must for any sparkling cocktail.

GIN

When working with gin to make a cocktail, you want to use its powerful, herbal, and woodsy nature to your advantage. You don't want to try and hide it, as it will take too much effort, and likely leave you with a drink that tastes clumsy, inarticulate. Instead, you want to highlight its character as best you can, either surrounding it with floral, herbal, and vegetal elements, setting it off with fruity and spicy elements, or leaning upon gin's most reliable partners—citrus, vermouth, and bitters. Gin's strong flavor forces you to keep an important rule in cocktail making front of mind—it is always best to err on the side of simplicity with your creations. You'll see some exceptions to that approach here, as the leaders of the craft cocktail movement live to break such rules. But you will not see any cocktails where gin's strong backbone is saddled with too much to carry.

GLASSWARE: Rocks glass
GARNISH: Cocktail onions

NO TRUE SCOTSMAN

The distillery boom has produced a number of unique spirits that are able to turn classic recipes into something entirely new. We see that in the No True Scotsman, where The Botanist's Islay Gin and Lo-Fi's exceptional vermouth pair to reinterpret the Dirty Martini.

2 oz. The Botanist Islay Dry Gin

1 oz. Lo-Fi Dry Vermouth

¼ oz. olive brine

2 dashes of Berg & Hauck's Original Celery Bitters

1. Place all of the ingredients in a cocktail shaker, fill it two-thirds of the way with ice, and shake until chilled.

2. Strain the cocktail over ice into the rocks glass, garnish with cocktail onions, and enjoy.

GLASSWARE: Double rocks glass

GARNISH: Long strip of orange peel

THE CHURCH

The framework of the Negroni offers the imaginative mixologist ample room to play around in, as The Church proves. The Campari is swapped out for bright-but-still-bitter Aperol, and the vermouth is exchanged for Cocchi Americano, which is similarly herbal and aromatic, but not so heavy-handed. As Cocchi Americano is also citrusy, the addition of lemon juice ties everything together, and further brightens this brilliant take on a classic.

||||||||||||||||||||||||||||||||||||||||||||||||||||||||||||||||||||||||||||||||||||||||||||||||||||||||||||||||||||||||||||||||||||||||

1 oz. Aperol

1 oz. City of London Gin

1 oz. fresh lemon juice

½ oz. Demerara Syrup (see recipe)

½ oz. Cocchi Americano

1. Place all of the ingredients in a cocktail shaker, fill it two-thirds of the way with ice, and shake until chilled.

2. Double-strain the cocktail over a large ice cube into the double rocks glass, garnish with the strip of orange peel, and enjoy.

DEMERARA SYRUP: Place 1 cup water in a saucepan and bring it to a boil. Add ½ cup demerara sugar and 1½ cups sugar and stir until they have dissolved. Remove the pan from heat and let the syrup cool completely before using or storing.

GLASSWARE: Collins glass
GARNISH: 2 or 3 nori sheets, shredded

SEA COLLINS

A Tom Collins that looks to the ocean for inspiration. Oakland Spirits Company's Automatic Sea Gin is packed with foraged nori, lemongrass, and some other elements of coastal terroir, making it the ideal spirit to serve as the drink's anchor.

2 oz. Oakland Spirits Company Automatic Sea Gin

¾ oz. Seaweed-Infused Honey (see recipe)

½ oz. fresh lemon juice

½ oz. fresh lime juice

4 dashes of chamomile tincture

Soda water, to top

1. Place all of the ingredients, except for the soda water, in a cocktail shaker, fill it two-thirds of the way with ice, and shake until chilled.

2. Double-strain into the Collins glass, top with soda water, and gently stir.

3. Garnish with the shredded nori and enjoy.

SEAWEED-INFUSED HONEY: Place ½ cup honey and ½ cup water in a mason jar and stir until well combined. Add dried nori and let the mixture sit at room temperature for 3 hours. Strain before using or storing, making sure to press down on the nori to extract as much liquid and flavor as possible.

GLASSWARE: Collins glass
GARNISH: Peychaud's Bitters, freshly grated nutmeg, fresh mint, grapefruit twist

ASYLUM HARBOR

Martin Cate, the tiki enthusiast, rum aficionado, and James Beard Award winner behind the world-renowned Smugglers Cove in San Francisco, is also the brains behind another popular San Francisco bar, Whitechapel, where gin is the spirit that stands in the spotlight. The Asylum Harbor is one of the early returns from this project, and further cements Cate as one of contemporary mixology's brightest lights.

1¼ oz. Damrak Gin

½ oz. Bénédictine

¼ oz. almond liqueur

1 bar spoon of St. Elizabeth Allspice Dram

½ oz. Ginger Syrup (see recipe)

½ oz. passion fruit puree

½ oz. fresh lime juice

¾ oz. grapefruit juice

1. Place all of the ingredients in a cocktail shaker, fill it two-thirds of the way with ice, and shake until chilled.

2. Strain over ice into the Collins glass, garnish with the bitters, nutmeg, fresh mint, and grapefruit twist, and enjoy.

GINGER SYRUP: Place 1 cup water and 1 cup sugar in a saucepan and bring the mixture to a boil, stirring to dissolve the sugar. Add a peeled 1-inch piece of fresh ginger, remove the pan from heat, and let the syrup cool completely. Strain before using or storing.

GLASSWARE: Coupe
GARNISH: Chamomile blossoms, ground freeze-dried raspberries

CIRCE'S KISS

Aquafaba, the liquid that results from cooking chickpeas, has become a go-to in the drinks industry, as it can ably stand in for egg white while also removing any cause for health concerns.

1½ oz. gin

¼ oz. absinthe

¾ oz. Chamomile Syrup (see recipe)

1 oz. coconut milk

½ oz. aquafaba

1. Place all of the ingredients in a cocktail shaker, fill it two-thirds of the way with ice, and shake until chilled.

2. Strain the cocktail into the coupe, garnish with chamomile blossoms and ground freeze-dried raspberries, and enjoy.

   CHAMOMILE SYRUP: Add 1 tablespoon of chamomile blossoms or 2 bags of chamomile tea to Simple Syrup (see page 40) after the sugar has dissolved. Let the syrup cool and strain before using or storing in the refrigerator.

GLASSWARE: Rocks glass

GARNISH: Strip of orange peel

NEGRONI CAFFE

Mr Black's Coffee Liqueur has become an increasingly popular spirit with great bartenders, as it does not shy away from the bitter element that is coffee's signature characteristic, while also playing up the notes of vanilla and dark chocolate that are the marks of a quality roaster.

‖‖

1 oz. The Botanist Islay Dry Gin

½ oz. Espresso-Infused Campari (see recipe)

½ oz. sweet vermouth

¾ oz. Mr Black Coffee Liqueur

Dash of Fee Brothers Aztec Chocolate Bitters

1. Place all of the ingredients in a cocktail shaker, fill it two-thirds of the way with ice, and shake until chilled.

2. Strain into the rocks glass, garnish with the strip of orange peel, and enjoy.

ESPRESSO-INFUSED CAMPARI: Place 2 tablespoons espresso beans and a 750 ml bottle of Campari in a large mason jar and let the mixture steep for 3 hours. Strain before using or storing.

ORGEAT: Preheat the oven to 400°F. Place 2 cups almonds on a baking sheet, place them in the oven, and toast until they are fragrant, about 5 minutes. Remove the almonds from the oven and let them cool completely. Place the almonds in a food processor and pulse until they are a coarse meal. Set the almonds aside. Place 1 cup Demerara Syrup (see page 20) in a saucepan and warm it over medium heat. Add the almond meal, remove the pan from heat, and let the mixture steep for 6 hours. Strain the mixture through cheesecloth and discard the solids. Stir in 1 teaspoon orange blossom water and 2 oz. vodka and use immediately or store in the refrigerator.

GLASSWARE: Collins glass
GARNISH: Fresh mint, edible flower blossom

SLEEPING LOTUS

Orgeat—it's pronounced ore-zha—is a French, almond-based syrup that supplies an inimitable and irresistible floral quality wherever it appears, as well as a luxurious mouthfeel. It is a popular ingredient in tiki-inclined cocktails, such as the Sleeping Lotus.

3 fresh mint leaves

2 oz. gin

1 oz. Orgeat (see recipe)

¾ oz. fresh lemon juice

2 dashes of orange bitters

1. Place the mint in a cocktail shaker and muddle.

2. Add ice and the remaining ingredients and shake until chilled.

3. Fill the Collins glass with crushed ice and double-strain the cocktail over it.

4. Garnish with fresh mint and the edible flower blossom and enjoy.

GLASSWARE: Cocktail glass
GARNISH: Orange twist

HANKY PANKY

Originally published in *The Savoy Cocktail Book* in 1930, the Hanky Panky balances the sweetness of vermouth against the herbaceous quality of Fernet-Branca to create a delicious concoction with layers of flavor. A dash or two of Fernet is all you need—you don't want to risk overwhelming the delicate flavor of the gin—and it adds a wonderful, almost earthy quality to the cocktail.

1½ oz. London dry gin

1½ oz. sweet vermouth

2 dashes of Fernet-Branca

1. Place all of the ingredients in a cocktail shaker, fill it two-thirds of the way with ice, and shake until chilled.

2. Strain into the cocktail glass, garnish with the orange twist, and enjoy.

GLASSWARE: Coupe
GARNISH: Spritz of Green Chartreuse, edible flower petal

ANNE WITH AN E

Tart, dry, and austere, with a silky-smooth texture and an herbaceous nose, this is an impossibly elegant drink. That quality is drawn out even more by the finishing spritz of Green Chartreuse. And, since Chartreuse has become difficult to source over the course of the last year, this is a good drink to make sure you get your fix without using it all up at once.

2 oz. London dry gin

¾ oz. fresh lemon juice

½ oz. curaçao

½ oz. Honey Syrup (see recipe)

¾ oz. egg white

2 drops of 10 Percent Saline Solution (see recipe)

Large strip of grapefruit peel

1. Chill the coupe in the freezer.

2. Place all of the ingredients in a cocktail shaker and dry shake for 15 seconds.

3. Add ice and shake until chilled.

4. Double-strain the cocktail into the chilled coupe, spritz it with the Green Chartreuse, garnish with the edible flower petal, and enjoy.

HONEY SYRUP: Place 1½ cups water in a saucepan and bring it to a boil. Add 1½ cups honey and cook until it is just runny. Remove the pan from heat and let the syrup cool before using or storing in the refrigerator.

10 PERCENT SALINE SOLUTION: Place 1 oz. of salt in a measuring cup. Add warm water until you reach 10 oz. and the salt has dissolved. Let the solution cool before using or storing.

GLASSWARE: Cocktail glass
GARNISH: Citrus twist

CORPSE REVIVER #2

The Savoy Cocktail Book included a number of different variations on the Corpse Reviver, but Corpse Reviver #2 is the one that has stood the test of time. As its name implies, Corpse Reviver #2 is considered by many to be a hangover cure—and the sweet and sour combination of Cointreau, Lillet Blanc, and lemon juice will certainly revive your taste buds, if nothing else. It's another delicious cocktail that balances fruity and herbal notes, playing well off the botanicals found in gin.

1 oz. London dry gin

1 oz. Cointreau

1 oz. Lillet Blanc

1 oz. fresh lemon juice

Dash of absinthe

1. Place all of the ingredients in a cocktail shaker, fill it two-thirds of the way with ice, and shake until chilled.

2. Strain into the cocktail glass, garnish with the citrus twist, and enjoy.

GLASSWARE: Cocktail glass
GARNISH: Lemon twist

VESPER MARTINI

The signature drink of James Bond, the Vesper Martini was first introduced in the 1953 novel *Casino Royale*. It's a simple drink, but one that puts a refreshing spin on the classic Martini. The use of both gin and vodka is novel, and the inclusion of Lillet Blanc in place of dry vermouth gives the drink a lovely floral note. It's a sophisticated cocktail—one befitting of the world's most famous spy.

3 oz. London dry gin

1 oz. vodka

½ oz. Lillet Blanc

1. Place all of the ingredients in a mixing glass, fill it two-thirds of the way with ice, and stir until chilled.

2. Strain into the cocktail glass, garnish with the lemon twist, and enjoy.

GLASSWARE: Rocks glass
GARNISH: Pea shoots, edible flowers

FALLEN MADONNA

The Gin & Tonic is a classic, but the Fallen Madonna calls for the use of flat tonic water, removing the effervescence that would otherwise dominate the drink. The cocktail is sweetened with Simple Syrup and elevated with fresh lemon juice and aloe vera. The use of flat tonic water is surprisingly effective here: the bitterness of the tonic plays well with the earthy, herbal aloe vera, building layers of flavor atop the classic foundation.

1¾ oz. Tanqueray

1¼ oz. flat tonic water

2 teaspoons fresh lemon juice

1¾ teaspoons Simple Syrup (see recipe)

⅞ oz. fresh aloe vera gel

1. Place all of the ingredients in a cocktail shaker, fill it two-thirds of the way with ice, and shake until chilled.

2. Strain over ice into the rocks glass, garnish with pea shoots and edible flowers, and enjoy.

SIMPLE SYRUP: Place 1 cup sugar and 1 cup water in a saucepan and bring it to a boil, stirring to dissolve the sugar. Remove the pan from heat and let the syrup cool completely before using or storing.

GLASSWARE: Coupe
GARNISH: Strip of orange peel

MÓRIARTY

Named for Sherlock Holmes's famous adversary (and also for the Mór Irish Gin it contains), the Móriarty features a number of unique flavors that drinkers may not be familiar with. Picon Amer adds a subtle, dried orange flavor, while Suze is a bitter French aperitif. Balanced against the gin and sweet Cocchi Di Torino, they combine to create a more assertive and flavor-forward take on a Negroni.

⅞ oz. Mór Irish Gin

2 teaspoons Victory Gin

¾ oz. Cocchi Vermouth di Torino

2 teaspoons Suze

1 teaspoon Picon Amer

2 dashes of Angostura Bitters

1. Chill the coupe in the freezer.

2. Place all of the ingredients in a mixing glass, fill it two-thirds of the way with ice, and stir until chilled.

3. Strain into the chilled coupe, garnish with the strip of orange peel, and enjoy.

GLASSWARE: Hurricane glass
GARNISH: Pineapple slice, fresh mint, maraschino cherry

MIAMI SLING PUNCH

This drink does the impossible: it makes gin, a notoriously wintry spirit, feel positively tropical, adding a sharp, herbaceous note that goes surprisingly well with the sweet and fruity ingredients that make up the rest of the drink. And, like any "Sling" cocktail, it is striking to look at, with fresh, colorful garnishes bursting out of the Hurricane glass.

2 oz. gin

½ oz. Cherry Heering

½ oz. Reàl Ginger Syrup

2 oz. fresh pineapple juice

½ oz. Alamea Peach Brandy

¾ oz. fresh lime juice

2 dashes of Angostura Bitters

Club soda, to top

1. Place all of the ingredients in a cocktail shaker, fill it two-thirds of the way with ice, and shake until chilled.

2. Strain over crushed ice into the Hurricane glass and top with club soda.

3. Garnish with the slice of pineapple, fresh mint, and maraschino and enjoy.

GLASSWARE: Cocktail glass
GARNISH: Cucumber slice

THE BABY DILL

Gin, cucumber, lemon, and dill—it should come as little surprise that these ingredients play well together. You could almost consider the Baby Dill a "pickle Martini," though the use of both fresh cucumber and fresh dill keep the flavor profile refreshingly light.

2 cucumber slices

1 sprig of fresh dill

1¼ oz. 12 Bridges Gin

¼ oz. Simple Syrup
(see page 40)

¼ oz. fresh lemon juice

1. Chill the cocktail glass in the freezer.

2. Place the cucumber and dill in a cocktail shaker, add a bit of crushed ice, and muddle.

3. Add more ice and the remaining ingredients and shake until chilled.

4. Strain into the chilled cocktail glass, garnish with the cucumber slice, and enjoy.

VIOLET FIZZ

This fresh and tropical take on a Gin Fizz dazzles the taste buds with Passion Fruit Syrup, blue curaçao, and crème de violette layered over a gin base. The rich, blue hue is a feast for the eyes, as is the fizzy foam that sits atop the drink thanks to the inclusion of egg white and sparkling water.

2 oz. gin

¾ oz. fresh lemon juice

½ oz. crème de violette

¼ oz. Orgeat (see page 30)

¼ oz. Rich Simple Syrup (see recipe)

½ oz. egg white

¼ oz. Passion Fruit Syrup (see recipe)

¼ oz. blue curaçao

1 oz. sparkling water, chilled, to top

1. Place all of the ingredients, except for the sparkling water, in a cocktail shaker and dry shake for 10 seconds.

2. Add ice and shake vigorously until chilled.

3. Double-strain over 2 ice cubes into the Collins glass, top with the sparkling water, and enjoy.

RICH SIMPLE SYRUP: Place 2 cups sugar and 1 cup water in a saucepan and bring it to a boil, stirring to dissolve the sugar. Remove the pan from heat and let the syrup cool completely before using or storing.

PASSION FRUIT SYRUP: Place 1½ cups passion fruit puree and 1½ cups Demerara Syrup (see page 20) in a mason jar, seal it, and shake until combined. Use immediately or store in the refrigerator.

GLASSWARE: Wineglass

GARNISH: Lemon wheels, lime wheels, sprigs of fresh rosemary, sprigs of fresh thyme, Manzanilla olive, dried juniper berries

GIN + TONIC

How do you elevate a simple Gin & Tonic into something special? You start by using high-quality ingredients and you finish by using garnishes that perfectly complement the flavor profile of the drink. The inclusion of dried juniper berries is a particularly nice touch, further drawing out that element of the gin.

2 oz. gin

Fever-Tree Mediterranean Tonic, to taste

1. Pour the gin over ice into the wineglass.

2. Add tonic to taste, garnish with the lemon wheels, lime wheels, fresh rosemary, fresh thyme, Manzanilla olive, and dried juniper berries, and enjoy.

GLASSWARE: Cocktail glass
GARNISH: Fresh carrot frond

NIGHT VISION

Carrot juice in a cocktail? Let's go. A more vibrantly colored cocktail you'll never see, and the garnish of carrot frond adds a whimsical element to an already very fun cocktail. There are some complex flavors here, with gin and vermouth playing against the carrot and lemon juice, and the oloroso sherry and caraway tincture add subtle notes of their own. It's beautiful, craveable, and, most of all—unique.

1½ oz. Spirit Works Barrel Gin

1 oz. Fresh Carrot Juice Syrup (see recipe)

½ oz. fresh lemon juice

¼ oz. Bordiga Extra Dry Vermouth

2 dashes of oloroso sherry

2 dashes of Caraway Tincture (see recipe)

1. Chill the cocktail glass in the freezer.

2. Place all of the ingredients in a cocktail shaker, fill it two-thirds of the way with ice, and shake for 15 seconds.

3. Double-strain the cocktail into the chilled cocktail glass, garnish with the carrot frond, and enjoy.

FRESH CARROT JUICE SYRUP: Place 1 cup freshly pressed carrot juice and ½ cup Simple Syrup (see page 40) in a mason jar, stir to combine, and use as desired.

CARAWAY TINCTURE: Place 2 tablespoons caraway seeds and 4 oz. high-proof neutral grain alcohol in a mason jar and steep for at least 24 hours, shaking periodically. Strain before using or storing.

GLASSWARE: Tumbler
GARNISH: Thin slice of beet, edible rose petals

CRIMSON GARDEN

Gin mixes surprisingly well with a wide range of different vegetable juices, as shown in the Night Vision (see page 52). Here, fresh beet juice is the partner, creating an intriguingly pink cocktail with a rich, earthy flavor profile.

1½ oz. gin

½ oz. Rose Syrup
(see recipe)

1 oz. fresh beet juice

½ oz. fresh lemon juice

1½ to 2 oz. Q Spectacular
Tonic Water

1. Place all of the ingredients in a cocktail shaker, fill it two-thirds of the way with ice, and shake until chilled.

2. Pour the contents of the shaker into the tumbler, garnish with the slice of beet and rose petals, and enjoy.

ROSE SYRUP: Place 1 cup rose water in a saucepan and bring to a boil. Add 1 cup sugar and stir until it has dissolved. Remove the pan from heat and let the syrup cool completely before using or storing in the refrigerator.

GLASSWARE: Collins glass
GARNISH: Fresh dill

THE DILL MURRAY

Why is dill not used more often in cocktails? I don't have a good answer—it's a delicious ingredient that provides a perfect accent for so many different flavors. Here, it serves to draw out the freshness of cucumber juice, agave nectar, and lime, bringing a little something extra to an already tasty gin-based concoction.

1 sprig of fresh dill

2 oz. OOLA Gin

¾ oz. cucumber juice

½ oz. agave nectar

½ oz. fresh lime juice

3 dashes of Scrappy's Firewater Bitters

Domaine Ste. Michelle Brut, to top

1. Place the dill in a cocktail shaker and muddle it.

2. Add ice and all of the remaining ingredients, except the sparkling wine, and shake until chilled.

3. Strain over ice into the Collins glass and top with sparkling wine.

4. Garnish with fresh dill and enjoy.

GLASSWARE: Coupe
GARNISH: Black pepper

GARDEN PARTY

Gin, Aperol, lemon juice, and . . . red bell pepper? It might sound strange, but this unusual combination of flavors really works. Living up to its name, the Garden Party leans heavily on the garden, bringing it all together with a pinch of black pepper that gives a welcome bit of spice.

2 tablespoons chopped red bell pepper

2 oz. Hendrick's Gin

¾ oz. Aperol

¾ oz. fresh lemon juice

½ oz. Simple Syrup (see page 40)

1. Place the bell pepper in a cocktail shaker and muddle it.

2. Add ice and the remaining ingredients and shake until chilled.

3. Strain into the coupe, garnish with black pepper, and enjoy.

GLASSWARE: Wineglass
GARNISH: Cucumber slice, sprig of fresh rosemary, 3 slices of cherry tomato, 2 dashes of orange-flavored olive oil

CRYSTAL GAZPACHO

I've tasted gins with a wide range of different flavor profiles, but I have to say, Tomato Gin is a new one for me. This is a fascinating and complicated cocktail, but if you're feeling adventurous, the result is something truly fascinating. Is it delicious? Well, that will probably depend on how you feel about gazpacho—because the flavor profile of the drink certainly lives up to its name.

1 oz. Tomato Gin
(see page 60)

2 bar spoons Bread
St-Germain (see page 60)

2 bar spoons Noilly Prat Dry
Vermouth

½ oz. Tomato Shrub
(see page 60)

1⅓ oz. tonic water

1 oz. soda water

1. Place the gin, St-Germain, vermouth, and shrub in a cocktail shaker and dry shake for 15 seconds.

2. Pour over ice into the wineglass and top with the tonic water and soda water.

3. Garnish with the cucumber slice, fresh rosemary, slices of cherry tomato, and olive oil and enjoy.

TOMATO GIN: Place 6 cherry tomatoes with and 1 cup Beefeater 24 Gin in a blender and puree until smooth. Pour the mixture into a mason jar and chill in the refrigerator for 3 hours. Strain through a coffee filter before using or storing.

BREAD ST-GERMAIN: Place 1 oz. of French bread and 7 oz. St-Germain in a vacuum bag, vacuum seal it, and sous-vide at 140°F for 2 hours. Remove the vacuum bag from the water bath and let the mixture cool completely. Strain through a coffee filter before using or storing.

TOMATO SHRUB: Place 5 tomatoes in a blender and puree until smooth. Strain the puree through a coffee filter until you have 10 oz. of tomato water, leaving the puree overnight if necessary. Place the tomato water and 5 oz. sugar in a saucepan and bring it to a simmer over low heat, stirring to dissolve the sugar. Cook for 5 minutes, stir in a splash of white balsamic vinegar, and let the shrub cool completely before using or storing.

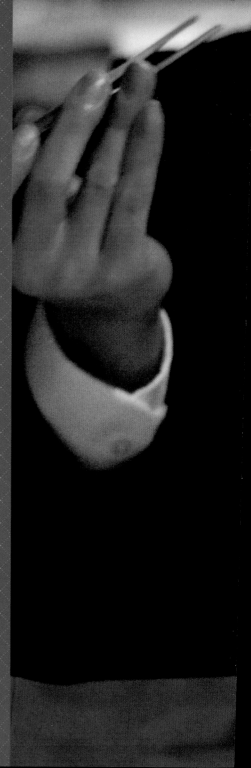

CRYSTAL GAZPACHO
see page 59

GLASSWARE: Coupe
GARNISH: Rose tincture

ROSEWATER SOUR

This cocktail is a work of art, both in terms of its construction and the resulting look. The Rosewater Mix is the real star of the show here, an ingredient that Texas bartender Pasha Morshedi initially kept a secret, before realizing it was too good withhold from the world.

||||||||||||||||||||||||||||||||||||||||||||||||||||||||||||||||||||||||||||||||||||||||||||||||||||||||||||||||||||||||||||||||||||

2 oz. floral gin (Uncle Val's Restorative or Hendrick's)

¾ oz. fresh lemon juice

¾ oz. Rosewater Mix (see recipe)

1 egg white

1. Place all of the ingredients in a cocktail shaker and dry shake for 15 seconds.

2. Add ice and shake until chilled.

3. Strain into the coupe, garnish with a few drops of rose tincture, and enjoy.

ROSEWATER MIX: Combine 2 parts Red Wine Syrup (see recipe) with 1 part Combier Rose Liqueur and 1 part Orgeat (see page 30).

RED WINE SYRUP: Combine equal parts caster (superfine) sugar and robust red wine and stir until the sugar has dissolved. Add cardamom tincture to taste and use or store in the refrigerator.

GLASSWARE: Cocktail glass
GARNISH: None

SHERLOCK

The freshness of the banana and lime plays well against the sweetness of the muscat liqueur. The maraschino liqueur might be the most important element in the entire cocktail, binding everything together.

|||||||||||||||||||||||||||||||||||||||||||||||||||||||||||||||||||||||||||||||||||||||||||||||||||||||||||||||||||||||||||||||||||||||||||

1 oz. No.3 London Dry Gin

½ oz. Mistia Muscat Liqueur

2 bar spoons Monin green banana syrup

2 bar spoons fresh lime juice

1 bar spoon Luxardo maraschino liqueur

1. Place all of the ingredients in a cocktail shaker, fill it two-thirds of the way with ice, and shake until chilled.

2. Strain into the cocktail glass and enjoy.

GLASSWARE: Cocktail glass
GARNISH: None

SHISUI

The matcha liqueur adds a little extra herbaceousness atop gin's powerful botanical elements, making this drink as refreshing as a stroll through the morning dew in early May.

¾ oz. Suntory Roku Gin

½ oz. Mistia Muscat Liqueur

2 bar spoons fresh lemon juice

1 bar spoon Ginger Syrup (see page 24)

1 bar spoon matcha liqueur

1. Place all of the ingredients in a cocktail shaker, fill it two-thirds of the way with ice, and shake vigorously until chilled.

2. Strain into the cocktail glass and enjoy.

GLASSWARE: Cocktail glass
GARNISH: Strip of lime peel

EVEN A TREE CAN SHED TEARS

Martini-like in terms of its simplicity, but the addition of Fauchon Tea Liqueur is a stroke of genius here, and its herbal qualities play off the gin in delightful—and delicious—ways. Tea liqueur isn't something most people have in their liquor cabinets at home, but this cocktail suggests maybe that should change.

||||||||||||||||||||||||||||||||||||||||||||||||||||||||||||||||||||||||||||||||||||||||||||||||||||||||||||||||||||||||||||||||||||||||||||||||||||||

1¼ oz. Herb-Infused
Tanqueray No. Ten
(see recipe)

½ oz. Mistia Muscat Liqueur

2 bar spoons Fauchon tea
liqueur

1 bar spoon fresh lemon
juice

1. Place all of the ingredients in a cocktail shaker, fill it two-thirds of the way with ice, and shake until chilled.

2. Strain into the cocktail glass, garnish with the strip of lime peel, and enjoy.

HERB-INFUSED TANQUERAY NO. TEN:
Take a fistful of herbs—half chamomile blossoms and half a mix of peppermint, cardamom, and lemongrass is a good place to start—and place it in a large mason jar. Add a 750 ml bottle of Tanqueray No. Ten gin and steep for 6 hours. Strain before using or storing.

WHISKEY

Whiskeys are slippery, multifaceted beasts. Even within a distinct category—bourbon, for example—there are a variety of tastes and flavors to be had. Evan Williams Single Barrel and Four Roses are both bourbons, but they do not taste the same. There are bourbons that will burn your face off—George T. Stagg, a cask-strength release that often tops 120 proof, comes to mind—and there are others that you would happily sip in your backyard. And that's just one branch of the whiskey tree. Take a quick tour through Scotch or Japanese whisky, and you will find yourself in a veritable forest of flavors.

That can make whiskey difficult to work with in cocktails—but this has, as you might expect, elicited some amazing work from the mixology movement. After all, it is dedicated to proving that anything can be put to good use if the imagination is playful enough and the execution is on point. As you'll see once you spend enough time with these recipes, any instance where the rules seem to be rigid is where there is actually the most freedom, the greatest chance to pull off something remarkable.

GLASSWARE: Cocktail glass
GARNISH: Edible flower blossoms

ANANDA SPRITZ

When you see spritz, you expect something that is light, simple, and refreshing. The Ananda Spritz is all of those things, but it takes a fascinating route to that destination, brilliantly incorporating darker-hued elements such as bourbon and amaro.

5 pineapple chunks

1½ oz. Knob Creek Bourbon

1 oz. Amaro Nonino

3 dashes of Angostura Bitters

½ oz. Demerara Syrup (see page 20)

½ oz. fresh lemon juice

½ oz. pineapple juice

¾ oz. sparkling wine

1. Place the pineapple in a cocktail shaker and muddle it.

2. Add all of the remaining ingredients, except for the sparkling wine, fill the shaker two-thirds of the way with ice, and shake until chilled.

3. Strain the cocktail into the cocktail glass and top with the sparkling wine.

4. Garnish with edible flower blossoms and enjoy.

GLASSWARE: Cocktail glass
GARNISH: None

FORTH & CLYDE

A delicate balance of bitter, sweet, sour, and heat dwells in the Forth & Clyde. That may seem like a lot to fit into one glass, but St-Germain, which is a master at making the complex seem a matter of course, is more than up to the task.

Honey, as needed

Red pepper flakes, to taste

1 oz. Maker's Mark Bourbon

1 oz. Hendrick's Gin

1 oz. St-Germain

1 oz. fresh lime juice

1. Chill the cocktail glass in the freezer.

2. Pour a nickel-sized quantity of honey into a cocktail shaker.

3. Add red pepper flakes and the remaining ingredients and stir until the honey has dissolved.

4. Add as much ice as you can fit into the shaker, and shake for 18 seconds.

5. Strain the cocktail into the chilled cocktail glass and enjoy.

GLASSWARE: Rocks glass
GARNISH: Strip of orange peel

COCOA PUFF OLD FASHIONED

It's easy to think of the Old Fashioned as a cocktail reserved for mature palates and leave it be. But what's the fun in that? By making a bold call back to the the sugary cereals of childhood, this classic gets a new lease on life, while losing none of its refinement.

2 oz. Cocoa Puff–Infused Bourbon (see recipe)

5 drops of white soy sauce

2 dashes of Bittermens Xocolatl Mole Bitters

¼ oz. Simple Syrup (see page 40)

1. Place all of the ingredients in a mixing glass, fill it two-thirds of the way with ice, and stir until chilled.

2. Strain over a large ice cube into the rocks glass, garnish with the strip of orange peel, and enjoy.

COCOA PUFF–INFUSED BOURBON: Place 1 box of Cocoa Puffs and a 750 ml bottle of bourbon in a large container and let the mixture steep for 1 day. Strain before using or storing.

GLASSWARE: Coupe
GARNISH: Strip of orange peel

MR. SMOOTH

This is a riff on the Vieux Carré, a classic New Orleans cocktail that was created at the famous Carousel Bar in the Monteleone Hotel. Between the bourbon, Cynar, and Demerara Syrup, there's plenty of luscious caramel notes to enjoy, and prove that the moniker is not just a clever nickname.

2 oz. bourbon

¼ oz. Cognac

¼ oz. Cynar

¼ oz. Demerara Syrup
(see page 20)

2 dashes of Angostura
Bitters

1. Place all of the ingredients in a mixing glass, fill it two-thirds of the way with ice, and stir until chilled.

2. Strain the cocktail into the coupe, garnish with the strip of orange peel, and enjoy.

GLASSWARE: Rocks glass
GARNISH: Dehydrated apple slice

UTOPIA

California's St. George Spirits has become one of the very best craft producers in the world, expertly fashioning everything from whiskey, gin, and brandy to shochu and bitters. Their Spiced Pear Liqueur is a must for your home bar, supplying the warming and delicate flavors present in a well-made pastry.

1½ oz. Redemption Rye Whiskey

½ oz. St. George Spiced Pear Liqueur

½ oz. Vanilla Syrup (see recipe)

2 dashes of Fee Brothers Black Walnut Bitters

1. Place all of the ingredients in a mixing glass, fill it two-thirds of the way with ice, and stir until chilled.

2. Strain the cocktail over a large ice cube into the rocks glass, garnish with the dehydrated apple slice, and enjoy.

VANILLA SYRUP: Place 1 cup water in a small saucepan and bring it to a boil. Add 2 cups sugar and stir until it has dissolved. Remove the pan from heat. Halve 1 vanilla bean and scrape the seeds into the syrup. Cut the vanilla bean pod into thirds and add the pieces to the syrup. Stir to combine, cover the pan, and let the mixture sit at room temperature for 12 hours. Strain the syrup through cheesecloth before using or storing in the refrigerator.

GLASSWARE: Rocks glass
GARNISH: Dehydrated banana slice

ALGORITHM OF THE NIGHT

Banana liqueur can be tough to procure in certain parts of the country, but the Algorithm of the Night shows that the capable mixologist is always prepared to find a workaround. Indeed, infusing the hazelnut liqueur Frangelico with actual bananas creates a concoction that works better with strong-flavored spirits like rye whiskey than any of the banana liqueurs on the market.

2 oz. Ezra Brooks Rye Whiskey

Dash of Dale DeGroff's Pimento Aromatic Bitters

1 oz. Banana-Washed Frangelico (see recipe)

1. Place all of the ingredients in a mixing glass, fill it two-thirds of the way with ice, and stir until chilled.

2. Strain the cocktail over a large ice cube into the rocks glass, garnish with the dehydrated banana slice, and enjoy.

BANANA-WASHED FRANGELICO: For every liter of Frangelico, cut up 3 bananas and throw them into a vacuum bag along with the Frangelico and peels. Sous vide at 135°F, for 2 hours, then cool the mixture in an ice bath. Strain and bottle once the mixture is cool.

GLASSWARE: Coupe
GARNISH: Lemon twist

A STONE'S THROW

Once again, three proves to be the magic number in this simple, appealingly sweet-and-rich serve that owes its luscious texture to the Barolo Chinato and the memorable notes of pine and anise to the mastiha liqueur.

‖‖

1½ oz. Sazerac 6 Year Rye Whiskey

¾ oz. Cocchi Barolo Chinato

¾ oz. Skinos Mastiha Spirit Liqueur

1. Place all of the ingredients in a cocktail shaker. Fill another cocktail shaker with ice and place a julep strainer over the top.

2. Pour the mixture into the cocktail shaker containing the ice and then strain it back into the shaker containing no ice. Repeat this tossing process 3 or 4 times until the cocktail is chilled and diluted.

3. Strain the cocktail into the coupe, garnish with the lemon twist, and enjoy.

GLASSWARE: Coupe
GARNISH: Dehydrated lemon wheel

HIJINKS

As fans of single-malt Scotch tend toward excessive seriousness when it comes to their preferred spirit, it falls to the rest of us to get them to lighten up and think outside the box. They will no doubt recoil when you first suggest mixing Scotch into a cocktail, but upon encountering the delicate floral aromas that the Hijinks unlocks, they will no doubt undergo an attitude adjustment.

1½ oz. Glenmorangie X Scotch Whisky

¾ oz. Lustau Fino Sherry

¾ oz. Chamomile Syrup (see page 27)

½ oz. fresh lemon juice

1. Place all of the ingredients in a cocktail shaker, fill it two-thirds of the way with ice, and shake until chilled.

2. Strain the cocktail into the coupe, garnish with the dehydrated lemon wheel, and enjoy.

GLASSWARE: Double rocks glass
GARNISH: Green tea–washed ginger candy

OTIUM

The Otium is an all-out celebration of Japanese products and flavors, resulting in a beautifully balanced, smoky-yet-sweet drink that forces you to slow down and carefully consider every sip.

‖‖

1½ oz. Hibiki Harmony Whisky

¼ oz. Toki Suntory Whisky

¼ oz. L'Orgeat Almond Liqueur

¾ oz. fresh lemon juice

½ oz. Honey Syrup (see page 35)

1 bar spoon yuzu juice extract

2 dashes of Miracle Mile Yuzu Bitters

1. Place all of the ingredients in a cocktail shaker, fill it two-thirds of the way with ice, and shake until chilled.

2. Double-strain over a large ice cube into the double rocks glass, garnish with the ginger candy, and enjoy.

GLASSWARE: Rocks glass
GARNISH: Fresh mint

QUARTER TANK OF GASOLINE

You might think you are unfamiliar with the flavor of sassafras, but if you've ever had root beer, you know what to expect. Here, it lends that recognizable vanilla and anise–tinged wintergreen quality to this innovative take on the Whiskey Smash.

2 oz. Nelson's Green Brier Tennessee Whiskey

1 oz. Sassafras Syrup (see recipe)

½ oz. fresh lemon juice

1. Place all of the ingredients in a cocktail shaker, fill it two-thirds of the way with ice, and shake until chilled.

2. Strain the cocktail over ice into the rocks glass, garnish with fresh mint, and enjoy.

SASSAFRAS SYRUP: Place 3 sprigs of fresh mint, the zest of 2 lemons, and 1½ cups Simple Syrup (see page 40) in a large mason jar and muddle. Add 1½ cups sassafras tea concentrate, shake to combine, and chill the syrup in the refrigerator overnight before using.

GLASSWARE: Rocks glass
GARNISH: 4 drops of cherry gelatin

CUBISM

Now, here's a unique cocktail—one that is as much about presentation as it is about taste. Bourbon, Cognac, rum, and Fernet-Branca Menta might not seem like they go together at first glance, but, like a Picasso painting, there is far more to this cocktail than meets the eye. The inclusion of cherry gelatin along the rim of the glass might seem unnecessary at first, but it adds to the whimsical feel of a cocktail that is as fun to look at as it is to drink.

||||||||||||||||||||||||||||||||||||||||||||||||||||||||||||||||||||||||||||||||||||||||||||||||||||||||||||||||||||

1 oz. Bulleit Bourbon

2 teaspoons Cognac

2 teaspoons Diplomático Reserva Rum

2 teaspoons Simple Syrup (see page 40)

1 teaspoon Fernet-Branca Menta

1 strip of lemon zest

1. Place all of the ingredients in a mixing glass, fill it two-thirds of the way with ice, and stir until chilled.

2. Strain over a large ice cube into the rocks glass, apply the four drops of cherry gelatin just below the rim of the glass, making sure they are parallel to the rim, and enjoy.

GLASSWARE: Goblet
GARNISH: Baby corn, cornflower

FIRE STAR PUNCH

This cocktail takes a bit of work, but the result is well worth it. And while the inclusion of hibiscus tea, Red Pepper Syrup, and a Citric Acid Solution might raise some eyebrows, it's hard to argue with a cocktail as flavorful and vibrant as this one. Inspired by the foods astronauts might someday eat on Mars (the "Fire Star"), it's a space age cocktail made from surprisingly grounded ingredients.

1 oz. Mellow Corn Whiskey

1 oz. Wild Turkey Rye Whiskey

¾ oz. Martini & Rossi Riserva Speciale Bubino

½ oz. Martini & Rossi Bitter

1¼ oz. iced hibiscus tea

½ oz. Red Pepper Syrup (see recipe)

½ oz. Citric Acid Solution (see recipe)

1. Place all of the ingredients in a mixing glass and fill it two-thirds of the way with ice. Using another mixing glass, utilize the Cuban roll method: pour the cocktail back and forth between the glasses three times; the more distance between your glasses, the better.

2. Place a large ice cube in the goblet and strain the cocktail over it.

3. Garnish with the baby corn and cornflower and enjoy.

RED PEPPER SYRUP: Place 9 oz. water in a saucepan and bring it to a boil. Add 2 chopped red bell peppers and 17½ oz. demerara sugar and stir until the sugar has dissolved. Remove the pan from heat and let the syrup cool completely. Pour the mixture, without straining, into a mason jar and chill it in the refrigerator overnight. Strain the syrup before using or storing.

CITRIC ACID SOLUTION: Place 10 oz. water and ½ oz. citric acid in a mason jar and stir until the citric acid has dissolved. Use as desired.

GLASSWARE: Coupe
GARNISH: Lemon twist

MIND MAPS

Drinks featuring Scotch should always be about accentuating and elevating the flavors present in the whisky, not hiding them—and Mind Maps executes that theory perfectly, spotlighting the pear and the chocolate.

1¾ oz. blended Scotch whisky

2 teaspoons amontillado sherry

1½ teaspoons pear liqueur

1 teaspoon white crème de cacao

1 teaspoon Cointreau

½ teaspoon Demerara Syrup (see page 20)

2 dashes of Angostura Bitters

1. Chill the coupe in the freezer.

2. Place all of the ingredients in the chilled coupe and stir to combine.

3. Garnish with the lemon twist and enjoy.

GLASSWARE: Tumbler
GARNISH: Orange slice

MANDARIN KISS

Bourbon and Mandarin Puree may seem an odd couple, but as anyone who has ever enjoyed a torched orange peel with an Old Fashioned can attest, whiskey and orange go together better than you might think. With a splash of soda water for fizz, this simple cocktail unites two disparate flavor profiles to create something beautiful—and eminently drinkable.

2 oz. Maker's Mark Bourbon

2 tablespoons Mandarin Puree (see recipe)

Splash of soda water

1. Place the bourbon and puree in a cocktail shaker, fill it two-thirds of the way with ice, and shake until chilled.

2. Pour the contents of the shaker into the tumbler and top with the soda water.

3. Garnish with the slice of orange and enjoy.

MANDARIN PUREE: Peel, segment, and, if necessary, seed 4 mandarin oranges. Place the oranges in a blender with 1 tablespoon sugar and 1 teaspoon fresh lemon juice and pulse until chopped. Puree until smooth, taste, and add more sugar or lemon juice as desired. Use immediately or store in the refrigerator.

GLASSWARE: Cocktail glass
GARNISH: Lemon twist

LOVE IN A HOPELESS PLACE

What appears to be a mish mash of your liquor cabinet's odds and ends is in fact a beautifully thought-out cocktail. Fruity and minty, crisp and silky, this refined serve is full of surprises, and much more fun than one would think at first glance.

|||||||||||||||||||||||||||||||||||||||||||||||||||||||||||||||||||||||||||||||||||||||||||||||||||||||||||||||

1½ oz. Suntory Toki Japanese Whisky

1 oz. Lillet Blanc

¼ oz. Giffard Abricot du Roussillon liqueur

¼ oz. Giffard Menthe-Pastille

2 dashes of Peychaud's Bitters

1. Chill the cocktail glass in the freezer.

2. Place all of the ingredients in a mixing glass, fill it two-thirds of the way with ice, and stir until chilled.

3. Strain into the chilled cocktail glass, garnish with the lemon twist, and enjoy.

GLASSWARE: Rocks glass
GARNISH: Spritz of Becherovka, strip of orange peel

TETON TANYA

A contemporary spin on the classic Boulevardier, where Aperol and Cynar stand in for the traditional Campari and sweet vermouth and grant the drink a spicier, brighter quality.

|||||||||||||||||||||||||||||||||||||||||||||||||||||||||||||||||||||||||||||||||||||||||||||||||||||||||||||||||||||||||||||||||||||||

1 oz. Aperol

1 oz. Cynar

1 oz. rye whiskey

1. Place all of the ingredients in a mixing glass, fill it two-thirds of the way with ice, and stir until chilled.

2. Strain over a large ice cube into the rocks glass, garnish with the spritz of Becherovka and strip of orange peel, and enjoy.

GLASSWARE: Nick & Nora glass and mini-carafe
GARNISH: 3 cocktail cherries, skewered

MANHATTAN AND A HALF

Tweaking the classic Manhattan formula with a house-made Sweet Vermouth Blend and two different types of bitters shows how much room to play classic cocktails provide the thoughtful mixologist.

|||||||||||||||||||||||||||||||||||||||||||||||||||||||||||||||||||||||||||||||||||||||||||||||||||||||||||||||||||||||||||||||||

3 oz. bottled-in-bond bourbon

1 oz. Sweet Vermouth Blend (see recipe)

5 dashes of Angostura Bitters

3 dashes of Regans' Orange Bitters

1. Chill the Nick & Nora glass in the freezer. Place ice in a small container or bowl and place the mini-carafe atop the ice.

2. Place all of the ingredients in a mixing glass, fill it two-thirds of the way with ice, and stir until chilled.

3. Strain the majority of the cocktail into the chilled Nick & Nora glass. Strain the rest of the cocktail into the mini-carafe.

4. Garnish the Nick & Nora glass with the skewered cherries and enjoy.

SWEET VERMOUTH BLEND: Combine 1 part Carpano Antica Formula Sweet Vermouth with Dolin Vermouth de Chambery Rouge. Use immediately or store in the refrigerator.

GLASSWARE: Collins glass
GARNISH: Fresh mint, lime wheel

QUEEN OF THE DAMNED

Hibiscus and lime take this whiskey and Cognac–based cocktail to new heights, while the addition of Amaro Nonino brings it back down to earth. This is an exercise in balance, with sweet, sour, tart, and bitter flavors all bouncing off one another to create a cocktail that dances across every part of the tongue.

1½ oz. rye whiskey

½ oz. Cognac

¾ oz. fresh lime juice

½ oz. Hibiscus Cordial (see recipe)

¼ oz. Amaro Nonino

1. Place all of the ingredients in a cocktail shaker, fill it two-thirds of the way with ice, and shake until chilled.

2. Strain over ice into the Collins glass, garnish with fresh mint and a lime wheel, and enjoy.

HIBISCUS CORDIAL: Bring 4 cups water to a boil in a saucepan and turn off the heat. Add 1 oz. hibiscus tea and steep for 10 minutes. Add 1 oz. peeled and sliced ginger, 2 cinnamon sticks, 6 allspice berries, 2 whole cloves, the zest of 1 lemon, and 3 cups sugar, and bring the mixture to a gentle simmer. Cook for 15 minutes, stirring to dissolve the sugar. Remove the pan from heat and let the mixture steep overnight. Strain before using or storing in the refrigerator.

GLASSWARE: Coupe
GARNISH: Strip of citrus peel

SONG REMAINS THE SAME

Robert Plant himself might struggle to hit the high notes this cocktail reaches. The peatiness of the Scotch whisky plays beautifully with the sweetness of cherry and honey, while the citrus notes of lemon and orange bring it all into perfect balance.

2 oz. Ardbeg Scotch whisky

½ oz. Cherry Heering

½ oz. fresh lemon juice

½ oz. Honey Syrup
(see page 35)

2 drops of Bittermens
Orange Cream Citrate

1. Place all of the ingredients in a cocktail shaker, fill it two-thirds of the way with ice, and shake until chilled.

2. Strain into the coupe, garnish with the strip of citrus peel, and enjoy.

GLASSWARE: Hurricane glass
GARNISH: Candied pineapple wedge, Luxardo maraschino cherry, tiki umbrella

THE ROBIN'S NEST

Whiskey, rum, lemon, pineapple, passion fruit, and more are all represented in this wonderfully tropical cocktail that bears a beautiful, sunset-like hue in the glass.

1 oz. Suntory Toki Japanese Whisky

½ oz. Plantation O.F.T.D. rum

½ oz. Cinnamon Syrup (see recipe)

½ oz. fresh lemon juice

¾ oz. pineapple juice

1 oz. Passion Fruit Honey (see recipe)

1 oz. cranberry juice

1. Place all of the ingredients, except for the cranberry juice, in a cocktail shaker, fill it two-thirds of the way with ice, and shake vigorously until chilled.

2. Fill the Hurricane glass with crushed ice, strain the cocktail over it, and top with the cranberry juice.

3. Garnish the cocktail with the candied pineapple wedge and maraschino cherry and enjoy.

CINNAMON SYRUP: Place 1 cup water and 2 cinnamon sticks in a saucepan and bring the mixture to a boil. Add 2 cups sugar and stir until it has dissolved. Remove the pan from heat, cover it, and let the mixture steep at room temperature for 12 hours. Strain the syrup through cheesecloth before using or storing.

PASSION FRUIT HONEY: Place 1 cup honey in a saucepan and warm it over medium heat until it is runny. Pour the honey into a mason jar, stir in 1 cup passion fruit puree, and let the mixture cool before using or storing in the refrigerator.

GLASSWARE: Coupe
GARNISH: Strip of orange peel

ONE WAY FLIGHT

A beautiful blend of very specific ingredients (I'm guessing most people don't have cachaça or L'Aperitivo Nonino sitting around in their liquor cabinets). The garnish of torched orange peel gives a toasty, caramelized quality to the concoction and creates a welcoming aroma that draws the drinker in before they even take their first sip. In a word, it's a masterpiece.

1½ oz. Redwood Empire Rye Whiskey

½ oz. cachaça

½ oz. L'Aperitivo Nonino

½ oz. Aurora Pedro Ximénez Sherry

2 dashes of Angostura Bitters

1. Place all of the ingredients in a mixing glass, fill it two-thirds of the way with ice, and stir until chilled.

2. Strain the cocktail into the coupe. Hold the strip of orange peel about 2 inches above a lit match for a couple of seconds. Twist and squeeze the peel over the lit match while holding it above the cocktail and taking care to avoid the flames

3. Rub the torched peel around the rim of the glass, drop it into the drink, and enjoy.

GLASSWARE: Rocks glass
GARNISH: Lime wheel, edible orchid, fresh mint

ALL TAI'D UP

The concept is simple: make a Mai Tai, but with bourbon. The result is delicious: a smoky, fruity, nutty cocktail that takes a classic recipe and elevates it into something new. The use of Maple & Pecan Falernum gives the drink a little extra sweetness, and the flavor of the pecan really shines through. It's an unusual—but welcome—complement to the drink's classic orange and lime flavors.

||||||||||||||||||||||||||||||||||||||||||||||||||||||||||||||||||||||||||||||||||||||||||||||||||||||||||||||||||||||||||||||||

1 banana leaf

2 oz. bourbon

1 oz. Maple & Pecan Falernum (see recipe)

½ oz. fresh orange juice

½ oz. fresh lime juice

½ oz. curaçao

1. Trim the banana leaf into a rectangle and place it on the bottom of the rocks glass. Fill the glass with pebble ice.

2. Combine the remaining ingredients in a cocktail shaker, fill it two-thirds of the way with ice, and shake until chilled.

3. Strain the cocktail over ice into the glass, garnish with the lime wheel, edible orchid, and fresh mint, and enjoy.

MAPLE & PECAN FALERNUM: Divide 2 cups toasted pecans between two large mason jars. Cover the pecans with water and let the mixture steep for 24 hours. Place 1½ cups sugar in a large container. Add the peel of 1 orange and the peel of 1 lime and muddle the mixture. Let the oleo saccharum sit for 24 hours. Place 2 cinnamon sticks, 10 whole cloves, 10 allspice berries, and 3 star anise pods in a large saucepan and toast them over medium-high heat for 1 minute, shaking the pan frequently. Add the pecan mixtures, oleo saccharum, and ¼ cup chopped ginger to the pan and reduce the heat to medium. Bring the mixture to a simmer and cook for 30 minutes, taking care not to burn the sugar or let the mixture boil over. Strain the syrup and place it in a clean sauce-pan. Warm the syrup over medium-low heat, add 1 cup maple sugar, 1 cup maple syrup, 2 tablespoons orange juice, and 2 tablespoons fresh lime juice, and cook until the maple flavor is to your liking, stirring to dissolve the sugar. Remove the pan from heat and let the mixture cool. Strain the mixture into a large mason jar. Add 1 oz. 151-proof rum for every 5 oz. of the mixture. Cover the jar, shake to combine, and use immediately or store at room temperature.

GLASSWARE: Stemless wineglass
GARNISH: Berry Compote (see recipe), long strip of lemon peel

BERRY WHITE

A cocktail as smooth as the voice of the man it's named for. The Wild Berry Cordial makes a big difference here, elevating what would otherwise be a very straightforward mix of whiskey, lemon, and orange flavors into something more akin to a fruit punch. Both colorful and delicious, this is a drink you'll probably want to prepare again and again.

2 oz. bourbon

¾ oz. fresh orange juice

½ oz. fresh lemon juice

½ oz. Demerara Syrup (see page 20)

1 oz. Wild Berry Cordial (see recipe)

1. Place all of the ingredients in a cocktail shaker, fill it two-thirds of the way with ice, and shake until chilled.

2. Double-strain into the wineglass, garnish with the Berry Compote and long strip of lemon peel, and enjoy.

WILD BERRY CORDIAL: Place 2 pints blueberries, 1 pint blackberries, 1 pint raspberries, 3 cups brown sugar, and 1 cup bourbon in a saucepan and bring it to a boil. Cook until the berries start to break down, remove the pan from heat, and let the cordial cool completely. Double-strain before using or storing.

BERRY COMPOTE: Place 1 cup mixed berries in a mason jar, cover them with Cognac, and let the berries macerate for 8 hours. Strain before using or storing in the refrigerator.

GLASSWARE: Cocktail glass
GARNISH: Szechuan peppercorns

SZECHUAN SOUR

Lemon and pepper is a classic combination, so perhaps it should come as little surprise that Szechuan peppercorns make for the perfect addition to a whiskey sour. A concoction that is certain to make your taste buds tingle.

2 oz. whiskey

1 oz. fresh lemon juice

1 oz. Szechuan Peppercorn Syrup (see recipe)

1 large egg white (optional)

1. If using egg white, place all of the ingredients in a cocktail shaker without ice and shake for 60 seconds. Add ice to the shaker and shake again for 30 seconds. Strain into the cocktail glass, garnish with Szechuan peppercorns, and enjoy.

2. If not using egg white, place all of the ingredients in a cocktail shaker, fill it two-thirds of the way with ice, and shake until chilled. Strain into the cocktail class, garnish with Szechuan peppercorns, and enjoy.

SZECHUAN PEPPERCORN SYRUP: Grind 1 tablespoon Szechuan peppercorns. Place ½ cup sugar and ½ cup boiling water in a mason jar and stir to combine. Add the ground peppercorns and steep for 20 minutes. Strain and let the syrup cool completely before using or storing.

GLASSWARE: Collins glass
GARNISH: Strip of lemon peel

THIRD COAST MULE

Coastal areas in the US that are neither East Coast nor West Coast are sometimes referred to by the somewhat tongue-in-cheek moniker "Third Coast." Houston's location on the Gulf of Mexico certainly qualifies, and this cheekily named cocktail brings a whole mess of Texas flavor. Yellow Rose Distilling was Houston's first legal whiskey distillery, and it makes sense to honor that heritage with a Texas-sized twist on an old classic.

||||||||||||||||||||||||||||||||||||||||||||||||||||||||||||||||||||||||||||||||||||||||||||||||||||||||||||||||||||||||||||||

1½ oz. Yellow Rose Premium American Whiskey

¾ oz. fresh lemon juice

¾ oz. Simple Syrup (see page 40)

½ oz. coconut water

1½ oz. ginger beer

1. Place the whiskey, lemon juice, and syrup in a cocktail shaker, fill it two-thirds of the way with ice, and shake until chilled.

2. Strain over ice into the Collins glass and top with the coconut water and ginger beer.

3. Express the strip of lemon peel over the cocktail, garnish the drink with it, and enjoy.

GLASSWARE: Nick & Nora glass

GARNISH: 3 spritzes of Islay Scotch whisky, fresh tarragon, strip of grapefruit peel

TARRAGUEUR

The Tarragueur was created by Austin's bar star Justin Lavenue, who has graced the cover of *GQ* and been named Bombay Sapphire's Most Imaginative Bartender. It serves as the perfect representation of his skill when it comes to balancing strong flavors. Whiskey and grapefruit juice are a wonderful combination, and the addition of Honey Syrup, grapefruit peel, and tarragon leaves introduce sweet, sour, bitter, and herbal flavors that pull your tongue in several directions at once.

1½ oz. Texas whiskey (Balcones Single Malt or Balcones True Blue Cask Strength preferred)

1 oz. ruby red grapefruit juice

½ oz. Honey Syrup (see page 35)

Strip of grapefruit peel

8 fresh tarragon leaves

Dash of 10 Percent Saline Solution (see page 35)

1. Place all of the ingredients in a cocktail shaker and muddle.

2. Add 1 large ice cube and shake until chilled.

3. Strain into the Nick & Nora glass, spritz the cocktail with Islay Scotch, garnish with fresh tarragon and the strip of grapefruit peel, and enjoy.

GLASSWARE: Cocktail glass
GARNISH: None

PANTHEON

Scotch whisky is the primary ingredient here, but creator Daisuke Ito sees it as Bénédictine modified with Scotch and lemon juice. That's fair—Bénédictine has a unique, honey-like flavor that is sweet without becoming medicinal like other, similar liqueurs.

||||||||||||||||||||||||||||||||||||||||||||||||||||||||||||||||||||||||||||||||||||||||||||||||||||||||||||||||||||||||||||||||

1 oz. Scotch whisky

½ oz. Bénédictine

½ oz. fresh lemon juice

1. Place all of the ingredients in a cocktail shaker, fill it two-thirds of the way with ice, and shake until chilled.

2. Strain into the cocktail glass and enjoy.

GLASSWARE: Cocktail glass
GARNISH: Cinnamon-dusted dried rosebud

LAUGH

The Laugh is truly beautiful to look at. The cinnamon-dusted dried rosebud that garnishes the cocktail sits atop its lovely, reddish-pink body and invites the drinker in. Scotch is the foundation here, but a bevy of other delicate flavors make themselves known, including amazake, apple, and loose-leaf ruby orange tea. A cocktail so perfect and well balanced that you almost won't want to drink it.

1⅓ oz. Johnnie Walker Gold Label Scotch Whisky

⅔ oz. Amazake Falernum (see recipe)

½ oz. Apple Pie Juice (see recipe)

1 bar spoon fresh lemon juice

1 bar spoon loose-leaf ruby orange tea

Dash of Bob's Orange & Mandarin Bitters

1. Place all of the ingredients in a cocktail shaker, fill it two-thirds of the way with ice, and shake until chilled.

2. Strain into the cocktail glass, garnish with the cinnamon-dusted dried rosebud, and enjoy.

AMAZAKE FALERNUM: Place 1 cup amazake, 1 cup sugar, 1 cinnamon stick, ¼ vanilla bean, ½ teaspoon cardamom pods, ¼ teaspoon whole cloves, 2 lemon slices, and 2 lime slices in a saucepan and bring to a simmer over medium heat, stirring to dissolve the sugar. Remove the pan from heat and let the falernum cool completely. Strain before using or storing.

APPLE PIE JUICE: Place 10 oz. apple juice, ¼ teaspoon cinnamon, and ½ vanilla bean in a saucepan and bring to a boil over medium-high heat. Cook until the mixture has reduced by half. Remove the pan from heat and let the mixture cool completely. Strain before using or storing.

GLASSWARE: Cocktail glass
GARNISH: None

TAMAYURA

Whisky, green tea, and white chocolate go together great, and the inclusion of a spoonful of cream gives this cocktail a real dessert-like feel. It's easy to make and even easier to drink, and it will definitely make you wonder why you don't keep green tea liqueur in your liquor cabinet at home.

1 oz. Suntory Hibiki Blended Whisky

½ oz. Suntory Hermes Green Tea Liqueur

⅓ oz. white chocolate liqueur

1 bar spoon heavy cream

1. Place all of the ingredients in a cocktail shaker, fill it two-thirds of the way with ice, and shake until chilled.

2. Strain into the cocktail glass and enjoy.

GLASSWARE: Rocks glass
GARNISH: None

JAZERAC

There's nothing too fancy going on here: the Sazerac's beauty is in its simplicity, and the Jazerac honors that by not straying too far from the original recipe. The big draw here is the homemade Yuzu Peel Bitters, which the inventive mixologist will find no shortage of uses for.

Absinthe, to rinse

1⅓ oz. Nikka From The Barrel Whisky

⅔ oz. Nikka XO Deluxe Brandy

2 bar spoons Simple Syrup (see page 40)

1 bar spoon Yuzu Peel Bitters (see recipe)

1. Rinse the rocks glass with absinthe and discard any excess.

2. Place two large ice cubes in the glass and stir. Remove the top cube and discard it.

3. Add the remaining ingredients and stir until chilled. Remove the remaining ice cube and discard it.

YUZU PEEL BITTERS: Peel a yuzu and dry the peel—placing it in front of a running fan for a day or two is a good way to get the proper level of dryness. Cram as much of the peel as possible into a jar and fill it with high-proof vodka. Let the mixture steep for 6 months. Strain before using or storing.

TEQUILA & MEZCAL

When using tequila in a cocktail, there's really only one rule that you need to adhere to: do not use any expression that is less than 100 percent blue agave—also known as a mixto. Since they are cheaper to produce, there are many more mixto brands on the market than there are pure agave brands. Legally, these mixto tequilas must be made with at least 51 percent pure blue agave sugar. The other portion of the sugars can be from non-agave sources, like sugarcane, which will affect the taste of the spirit in a negative fashion.

Mezcal is a little different— since it is far more of a craft spirit than tequila, meaning that you can expect a wide range of flavors among the various producers and expressions. That's not to say don't experiment—feel free to try mixing any mezcal you enjoy, but Del Maguey's Vida offering is a good fallback, since it was designed in response to bartenders asking the company to make something that was more amenable to crafting cocktails.

GLASSWARE: Rocks glass
GARNISH: Orange twist

OAXACA OLD FASHIONED

Created by agave spirits evangelist Phil Ward at the infamous Death & Co, this is the drink that got the cocktail world excited about mezcal. Don't be afraid to experiment with the type of bitters employed in this one—in an evolved version Ward went with Bittermens Xocolatl Mole Bitters—or to go all in on a mezcal-only version.

||||||||||||||||||||||||||||||||||||||||||||||||||||||||||||||||||||||||||||||||||||||||||||||||||||||||||||||||||||||||||||||||

1½ oz. reposado tequila

½ oz. mezcal

2 dashes of Angostura Bitters

1 bar spoon agave nectar

1. Place a large ice cube in the rocks glass. Add all of the ingredients and stir until chilled.

2. Hold the strip of orange peel about 2 inches above a lit match for a couple of seconds. Twist and squeeze the peel over the lit match while holding it above the cocktail and taking care to avoid the flames.

3. Rub the torched peel around the rim of the glass, drop it into the drink, and enjoy.

GLASSWARE: Coupe
GARNISH: Strip of orange peel

L & N

Reposado translates to "rested," and is an indication that the tequila has spent some time—at least 2 months, usually less than a year—in a barrel. That brief respite is just enough to draw out the best characteristics of an agave-based spirit—spice, sweetness, earthiness—so that it becomes strong enough to stand as the backbone of a cocktail, while also playing well with others.

1½ oz. Cincoro Tequila Reposado

¾ oz. Honey & Basil Syrup (see recipe)

2 dashes of Angostura Bitters

Bittermens Xocolatl Mole Bitters, to taste

1. Place all of the ingredients in a cocktail shaker, fill it two-thirds of the way with ice, and shake until chilled.

2. Strain the cocktail into the coupe, garnish with the strip of orange peel, and enjoy.

   HONEY & BASIL SYRUP: Place 1 cup honey and 1 cup water in a saucepan and bring to a simmer, stirring until the honey has emulsified. Remove the pan from heat, add 2 handfuls of basil leaves, and let the mixture cool. Strain the syrup before using or storing in the refrigerator.

GLASSWARE: Rocks glass
GARNISH: Orange wedge

MR. KOTTER

While certainly eye-catching, the Hibiscus Ice Cubes are here for far more than aesthetic considerations. As they melt, they slowly infuse the cocktail with their juicy and tart flavor, making each sip a brand-new experience, and ensuring that this is a cocktail everyone will linger over.

2 oz. Tapatio Tequila

½ oz. Pierre Ferrand Dry Curaçao

1 oz. fresh lime juice

¼ oz. agave nectar

1. Place all of the ingredients in a cocktail shaker, fill it two-thirds of the way with ice, and shake vigorously until chilled.

2. Double-strain over a Hibiscus Ice Cube (see recipe) into the rocks glass, garnish with the orange wedge, and enjoy.

   HIBISCUS ICE CUBES: Place 8 cups water, 1 cup dried hibiscus blossoms, and an entire orange peel in a saucepan and bring to a boil. Remove the pan from heat and let the mixture steep for 3 hours. Strain, pour the strained liquid into ice molds, and freeze.

GLASSWARE: Collins glass
GARNISH: Grapefruit wheel, lime wheel, dehydrated grapefruit chip

GUERA

The tequila-and-mezcal boom has done wonders for the Paloma, elevating it onto cocktail menus all over the globe, and establishing it as the penultimate tequila cocktail, behind the Margarita. That increased respect and attention mean that the riffs, twists, and interesting takes on the classic formula are going to start pouring in, and among those that I've seen thus far, the Guera is the early leader in the clubhouse.

1½ oz. tequila

1 oz. grapefruit juice

¾ oz. fresh lime juice

¼ oz. Aperol

¼ oz. St-Germain

¼ oz. Thai Pepper Shrub (see recipe)

Fever-Tree Bitter Lemon Soda, to top

1. Place all of the ingredients, except for the soda, in the Collins glass, add ice, and stir until chilled.

2. Top with soda, garnish with the grapefruit wheel, lime wheel, and dehydrated grapefruit chip, and enjoy.

THAI PEPPER SHRUB: Place 4 chopped Thai chile peppers, ¼ cup cane vinegar, and ¼ cup cane sugar in a saucepan and bring to a boil. Cook for 5 minutes, remove the pan from heat, and let the shrub cool completely. Strain before using or storing.

GLASSWARE: Collins glass
GARNISH: Fresh mint

GHOST IN THE SHELL

The Ghost in the Shell provides a valuable lesson to the home bartender looking to step up their game—get familiar with sherry in all its forms, and then think of ways to incorporate them in your cocktail making. Amontillado's flavor is nutty with a hint of tobacco, making it a natural partner for the smoky mezcal.

1 oz. Del Maguey Vida
Mezcal

1 oz. amontillado sherry

¾ oz. fresh lime juice

½ oz. Orgeat (see page 30)

½ oz. Ginger Syrup
(see page 24)

1. Place all of the ingredients in a cocktail shaker, fill it two-thirds of the way with ice, and shake until chilled.

2. Fill the Collins glass with crushed ice and double-strain the cocktail over it.

3. Top with more crushed ice, garnish with fresh mint, and enjoy.

GLASSWARE: Collins glass
GARNISH: Fresh mint

OAXACAN BOTTLEROCKET

A tribute to the Queen's Park Swizzle, a proto-tiki drink that is believed to date back to the nineteenth century. Instead of the trio of rums that has become standard in that classic, the mezcal directs the proceedings into drier territory, and the chile-based syrup and falernum supply some welcome spice.

Handful of fresh mint

¾ oz. Del Maguey Vida Mezcal

¾ oz. Smith & Cross Rum

1 oz. fresh lime juice

¾ oz. Thai Chile & Basil Syrup (see recipe)

½ oz. falernum

½ oz. orange juice

Peychaud's Bitters, to top

1. Place the fresh mint at the bottom of the Collins glass and fill the glass with pebble ice.

2. Fill the glass with the remaining ingredients, except for the bitters, and top with more pebble ice.

3. Top with bitters until you see a nice red layer on the top of the drink. Garnish with additional fresh mint and enjoy.

THAI CHILE & BASIL SYRUP: Add ⅓ oz. of diced Thai chile pepper and one-quarter of a package of Thai basil to 2 cups of Simple Syrup (see page 40). Let the mixture steep in the refrigerator for 2 days and strain before using or storing.

GLASSWARE: Tumbler or cocktail glass
GARNISH: Wide lemon twist or grapefruit peel cone, and crushed pink peppercorns

PAMPLEMOUSSE AU POIVRE

H. Joseph Ehrmann won the 2018 Cocktail of the Year award with this cocktail at the San Francisco World Spirits Competition. After encountering its perfect balance of smoke, spice, and tanginess, you'll understand why.

2 oz. mezcal

1 oz. Giffard Crème de Pamplemousse

½ oz. Elixir de Poivre Cordial (see recipe)

½ oz. fresh lemon juice

Dash of The Bitter Truth Grapefruit Bitters

1. Place all of the ingredients in a cocktail shaker, fill it two-thirds of the way with ice, and shake until chilled.

2. Strain into the tumbler, either over crushed ice and garnished with a sprinkle of crushed pink peppercorns and a wide lemon twist, or up into a cocktail glass and garnished with a grapefruit peel cone filled with crushed pink peppercorns rested on the rim.

   ELIXIR DE POIVRE CORDIAL: Place 1 cup Stolen Heart vodka (120 proof), 1 tablespoon pink peppercorns, ¼ teaspoon Szechuan peppercorns, and ½ teaspoon coriander seeds in a mason jar, cover, and let the mixture sit at room temperature for 24 hours. Strain and then mix with Simple Syrup (see page 40) at a 1:1 ratio.

GLASSWARE: Double rocks glass
GARNISH: Dehydrated jalapeño slice

HOME IS WHERE THE HEAT IS

Tamarind possesses one of the most beguiling flavors on Earth, shifting from tart and citrusy to buttery and sweet as it travels over one's palate. That dynamic nature makes it a powerful cocktail ingredient, capable of taking something as simple as the framework for a Spicy Margarita into the stratosphere.

Lava salt, for the rim

Cumin, for the rim

1½ oz. Spicy Mezcal (see recipe)

¼ oz. Giffard Banane du Brésil

½ oz. fresh lime juice

½ oz. Manzanilla sherry

¾ oz. Tamarind Syrup (see recipe)

1. Place lava salt and cumin in a dish and stir to combine. Wet the rim of the double rocks glass and coat it with the mixture.

2. Place the remaining ingredients in a cocktail shaker, fill it two-thirds of the way with ice, and shake until chilled.

3. Strain over ice into the rimmed glass, garnish with the dehydrated slice of jalapeño, and enjoy.

SPICY MEZCAL: Place sliced jalapeño in a bottle of mezcal and let it steep for 24 hours—determine the amount of jalapeños and the length of time you steep the mixture based on your spice tolerance. Strain before using or storing, and reserve the leftover jalapeños to garnish other cocktails or serve as a boozy and yummy snack.

TAMARIND SYRUP: Place ¼ cup tamarind pulp, 1 cup water, and 1 cup sugar in a saucepan and bring to a simmer, stirring to dissolve the sugar and incorporate the tamarind. Remove the pan from heat and let the mixture cool completely. Strain before using or storing.

GLASSWARE: Ceramic bowl
GARNISH: Cornflower leaves

HAY ZEUS

The electric blue color of this drink might throw you for a loop, but make no mistake: the Hay Zeus is one tasty, refined concoction, thanks in large part to the Zeus Juice Cordial. Garnished with cornflower leaves, the vibrant blue-and-green hues of the cocktail make it seem like something out of science fiction—fittingly, the flavor is out of this world.

½ oz. Olmeca Altos Tequila

½ oz. fresh lime juice

1¾ oz. Zeus Juice Cordial
(see recipe)

1. Place all of the ingredients in a cocktail shaker, fill it two-thirds of the way with ice, and shake until chilled.

2. Place a large ice cube in the ceramic bowl and strain the cocktail over it.

3. Garnish with the cornflower leaves and enjoy.

   ZEUS JUICE CORDIAL: Place ⅜ oz. crushed hay, 5¼ oz. celery juice, and 3½ oz. caster (superfine) sugar in a blender and puree until smooth. Strain the mixture through cheesecloth and stir in ⅞ oz. Simple Syrup (see page 40), 1 cup mezcal, 3½ oz. blue wine (Gik is a trusted brand), ½ oz. 10 Percent Saline Solution (see page 35), and 2 drops of MSK Toasted Coconut Flavour Drops. Use immediately or store in the refrigerator.

GLASSWARE: Large coupe
GARNISH: Dehydrated pineapple slice

GLASS OFF

An elevated take on the Margarita that utilizes Aperol, pineapple juice, and absinthe alongside the traditional mezcal, lime juice, and sweetener. The result is a cocktail absolutely bursting with flavor, with the sweet-and-sour notes of the Aperol, lime, and pineapple taking this drink to new heights. The metaphorical cherry on top is the addition of egg white to create a gorgeous foam atop an already beautiful drink.

1 oz. mezcal

¾ oz. Aperol

⅞ oz. fresh lime juice

½ oz. Demerara Syrup
(see page 20)

1¼ oz. pineapple juice

3 dashes of absinthe

1 egg white

1. Place all of the ingredients in a cocktail shaker containing no ice and dry shake for 15 seconds.

2. Fill the shaker two-thirds of the way with ice and shake vigorously until chilled.

3. Double-strain the cocktail into the large coupe, garnish with the dehydrated pineapple slice, and enjoy.

GLASSWARE: Rocks glass
GARNISH: None

CANOE CLUB

Fresh fruit and smoky mezcal go together extremely well, and the Canoe Club cocktail highlights that fact perfectly. The bold blackberry flavor of crème de mure and the sour pucker of lime juice dance in perfect time to the smoky beat of the mezcal in this delicately crafted cocktail. It's the rare drink that I would recommend just as strongly to those who already love mezcal as I would to those just getting a taste for it.

1½ oz. mezcal

½ oz. crème de mure

¾ oz. Ginger & Serrano Syrup (see recipe)

½ oz. fresh lime juice

3 dashes of Peychaud's Bitters

1. Place all of the ingredients in a cocktail shaker, stir to combine, fill the shaker two-thirds of the way with ice, and shake vigorously until chilled.

2. Fill the rocks glass with crushed or pebble ice, strain the cocktail over it, and enjoy.

GINGER & SERRANO SYRUP: Place 2 cups sugar, 1 cup water, 3 chopped serrano chile peppers, and 2 large chopped pieces of ginger in a saucepan and bring to a simmer, stirring to dissolve the sugar. Cook for 10 minutes and strain the syrup into a mason jar. Let the syrup cool completely before using or storing in the refrigerator.

GLASSWARE: Coupe
GARNISH: Dehydrated lemon slice

THE FIFTH ELEMENT

Everyone loves avocado, but it takes a true visionary to use it in a cocktail. Jose Mendin, a Miami bartender, is one such visionary. The Fifth Element incorporates Avocado Mix with the tequila, lime, and agave you might find in a traditional Margarita, and tops it with an egg white foam for a truly unique cocktail. The richness of the avocado and egg white combine to create a smooth, velvety texture that goes down easy.

Citrus Salt (see recipe), for the rim

2 oz. Tequila Avión Silver

2 oz. Avocado Mix (see recipe)

¾ oz. fresh lime juice

½ oz. agave nectar

1 egg white

1. Wet the rim of the coupe and dip it into the Citrus Salt.

2. Place all of the remaining ingredients in a cocktail shaker, fill it two-thirds of the way with ice, and shake until chilled.

3. Strain the cocktail into the coupe, garnish with the dehydrated lemon slice, and enjoy.

AVOCADO MIX: Place the flesh of 3 avocados, 2 lbs. peeled and cored pineapple, and ¾ lb. cilantro in a blender and puree until smooth. Use immediately or store in the refrigerator.

CITRUS SALT: Place ½ cup salt, the zest of 2 lemons, and the zest of 2 limes in an airtight container and stir to combine. Use immediately or store at room temperature.

GLASSWARE: 1924 miniature cocktail glass or a Pousse Café glass
GARNISH: Orange twist, orange zest, and orange oil

SPEEDY GONZALES

Made primarily with tequila and dry vermouth, the Speedy Gonzales could be interpreted as a take on a tequila Martini. But the addition of Aperol, agave nectar, and chile pepper extract elevates this drink to something more, with the flavors all vying for your attention with every sip. You'll feel the burn from the chile extract at the back of your throat even as the sweet and sour notes of the vermouth and Aperol tantalize the tip of your tongue.

1⅜ oz. Gran Centenario Reposado Tequila

½ oz. Noilly Prat Dry Vermouth

⅜ oz. Aperol

1 teaspoon agave nectar

5 drops of chile pepper extract

1. Place all of the ingredients in a mixing glass and fill it two-thirds of the way with ice. Using another mixing glass, utilize the Cuban roll method: pour the cocktail back and forth between the glasses three times; the more distance between your glasses, the better.

2. Strain over 2 ice cubes into the chosen glass, garnish with the orange twist, orange zest, and orange oil, and enjoy.

GLASSWARE: Rocks glass
GARNISH: Chile peppers

LA MULA

This take on a tequila-based Mule is as fun to drink as it is to say. What elevates this particular interpretation is the inclusion of spice via the chiles. It's a drink that's not for the faint of heart—but one that will perfectly complement a spicy dish if you're a big fan of heat.

1½ oz. Olmeca Altos Tequila Plata

½ oz. Domaine de Canton

1 oz. fresh lime juice

4 slices of jalapeño chile pepper

4 oz. ginger beer, to top

1. Place all of the ingredients, except for the ginger beer, in a cocktail shaker, fill it two-thirds of the way with ice, and shake until chilled.

2. Double-strain over ice into the rocks glass and top with the ginger beer.

3. Garnish with chile peppers and enjoy.

GLASSWARE: Rocks glass
GARNISH: Fresh sage

SAGED BY THE BELL

This is a truly striking cocktail—in terms of both visuals and taste. The Spicy Hibiscus Syrup gives the drink a bright red hue, making the green of the sage leaf garnish stand out beautifully. The hibiscus tang shakes hands with the sour bite of the lime juice, adding a layer of complexity atop the drink's mellow tequila base.

2 oz. Hornitos Plata Tequila

¾ oz. fresh lime juice

1 oz. Spicy Hibiscus Syrup (see recipe)

3 to 4 fresh sage leaves

2 dashes of Fee Brothers Peach Bitters

1. Place all of the ingredients in a cocktail shaker, fill it two-thirds of the way with ice, and shake until chilled.

2. Double-strain over a large ice cube into the rocks glass, garnish with fresh sage, and enjoy.

SPICY HIBISCUS SYRUP: Place 2 cups sugar, 1 cup water, ½ cup dried hibiscus blossoms, and ¼ lemon drop chile pepper in a saucepan and bring to a boil, stirring to dissolve the sugar. Remove the pan from heat and let the mixture steep for 8 hours. Strain before using or storing.

GLASSWARE: Champagne flute
GARNISH: Fresh raspberries

FORMOSA FIZZ

The Formosa Fizz is bar star Jeffrey Morgenthaler's spin on the Clover Club, swapping in tequila for the gin and amplifying it with raspberry and lemon. Fresh egg white gives the cocktail the titular "Fizz," layering a delicious, velvety foam atop an already appealing beverage.

1½ oz. silver tequila

¾ oz. fresh lemon juice

½ oz. Raspberry Syrup (see recipe)

½ oz. egg white

¼ oz. Rich Simple Syrup (see page 48)

1½ oz. soda water, chilled

1. Place all of the ingredients, except for the soda water, in a cocktail shaker, fill it two-thirds of the way with ice, and shake until chilled and foamy.

2. Strain into the Champagne flute and top with the soda water.

3. Garnish with fresh raspberries and enjoy.

RASPBERRY SYRUP: Combine 500 grams raspberries and 500 grams sugar in a deep saucepan, then gently press down the mixture with the back of a fork. Let it macerate for 15 minutes, then add 500 ml water. Bring the mixture to just below a boil over medium heat. Remove the pan from heat and let the syrup cool for 30 minutes. Strain the syrup through a fine-mesh sieve or cheesecloth before using or storing in the refrigerator.

GLASSWARE: Nick & Nora glass
GARNISH: Lime wheel

PARALLELOGRAM

Thanks to all of the spicy elements, this is a versatile cocktail, one that could warm you up in the winter, or help you soak up the summer vibes. It's also an instructive serve: one of the easiest and most reliable ways to keep your cocktail game fresh is to always be on the lookout for new bitters. Bitter Ex, a company based out of Chicago, is one of many new outfits that are providing unique and imaginative tinctures for you to experiment with.

Guerrero rub, for the rim

1½ oz. silver tequila

¾ oz. Aperol

¾ oz. fresh lime juice

¼ oz. agave nectar

3 dashes of Bitter Ex Aromatic Bitters

6 dashes of Bitter Ex Hot Pepper Bitters

1. Wet the rim of the Nick & Nora glass and coat it with the rub.

2. Place the tequila, Aperol, lime juice, and agave nectar in a cocktail shaker, fill it two-thirds of the way with ice, and shake until chilled.

3. Strain the cocktail into the rimmed glass and top with the bitters.

4. Garnish with the lime wheel and enjoy.

GLASSWARE: Margarita coupe
GARNISH: Cucumber slice, fresh cilantro, jalapeño slices

JARDÍN FRESCO

There are two routes you can take here, depending on where you stand on spicy cocktails. But whichever path you choose, there is no escaping the drink's wonderfully refreshing vegetal quality, which is brought fully to life by the Prosecco float.

5 slices of cucumber

1 slice of jalapeño chile pepper (optional)

1 sprig of fresh cilantro

1½ oz. silver tequila

¾ oz. St-Germain

1 oz. fresh lime juice

2 oz. Prosecco, to float

1. Place the cucumber, jalapeño (if desired), and cilantro in a cocktail shaker and muddle.

2. Add ice and the tequila, St-Germain, and lime juice, shake until chilled, and double-strain the cocktail into the Margarita coupe.

3. Float the Prosecco on top of the cocktail, pouring over the back of a spoon. Garnish with the slice of cucumber, fresh cilantro, and jalapeño and enjoy.

GLASSWARE: Coupe
GARNISH: Edible flower

VIOLET SKIES

As you may have picked up on by now, I'm a sucker for a colorful cocktail. The Violet Skies lives up to its name—its purple/magenta color evokes nothing so much as an evening sunset over water. There's a lot going on in this cocktail. While the primary liquor is mezcal, gin and brandy also make appearances alongside coconut liqueur and crème de violette. Amidst all that booze, fresh lemon juice and grapefruit bitters add a citrusy element that lightens the drink just enough.

¾ oz. Butterfly Pea Flower–Infused Mezcal (see recipe)

½ oz. Hood River Distillers Lewis & Clark Lookout Gin

½ oz. Ventura Spirits Strawberry Brandy

¼ oz. Kalani Coconut Liqueur

¼ oz. Rothman & Winter Crème de Violette

½ oz. fresh lemon juice

2 dashes of Scrappy's Grapefruit Bitters

1. Chill the coupe in the freezer.

2. Place all of the ingredients in a cocktail shaker and dry shake for 10 seconds. Add ice and shake vigorously until chilled.

3. Double-strain into the chilled coupe, garnish with an edible flower, and enjoy.

BUTTERFLY PEA FLOWER–INFUSED MEZCAL: Place 2 tablespoons dried butterfly pea flowers and a 750 ml bottle of mezcal in a mason jar, shake vigorously, and steep for 3 hours. Strain before using or storing.

GLASSWARE: Coupe
GARNISH: Lemon twist

EL NACIONAL

Mezcal and mole go together just as well as you'd expect, and the addition of Campari, vermouth, and just a touch of Scotch makes for a fascinating mix of flavors. It's a unique, elegant cocktail perfect for sipping on a raw, rainy day.

1 oz. Del Maguey Vida Mezcal

1 oz. Campari

½ oz. Luxardo Amaro Abano

½ oz. dry vermouth

3 dashes of Bittermens Xocolatl Mole Bitters

Spritz of Ardbeg 5-Year Islay Scotch Whisky, to top

1. Place all of the ingredients, except for the Ardbeg, in a mixing glass, fill it two-thirds of the way with ice, and stir until chilled.

2. Strain the cocktail into the coupe and spritz it with the Ardbeg.

3. Garnish with the lemon twist and enjoy.

GLASSWARE: Cocktail glass

GARNISH: Strip of orange peel and/or brandied cherry

THE METRÓPOLI

One of tequila's strengths when it comes to cocktails is being a more-than-able stand-in for whiskey, which this tequila-based take on a Manhattan proves. The perfect balance of reposado, vermouth, and orange bitters makes this an easy sipper for a fall or winter afternoon.

2 oz. reposado tequila

1 oz. sweet vermouth

Dash of orange bitters

1. Chill the cocktail glass in the freezer.

2. Place all of the ingredients in a mixing glass, fill it two-thirds of the way with ice, and stir until chilled.

3. Strain into the chilled cocktail glass, garnish with the strip of orange peel and/or brandied cherry, and enjoy.

GLASSWARE: Rocks glass
GARNISH: Cucumber curl or apple slice

THE SMOKY GREEN GODDESS

With tequila, mezcal, and agave nectar all called for, the Smoky Green Goddess cocktail is all-in on agave. But the real star of this drink is the Green Goddess Juice, made from kale, apple, cucumber, and celery. Don't have a juicer at home? That's OK—just experiment with any similar flavors you have access to.

1 oz. silver tequila

½ oz. mezcal

½ oz. agave nectar

½ to ¾ oz. fresh lime juice

1 oz. Green Goddess Juice (see recipe)

Tiny pinch of sea salt

1. Place all of the ingredients in a cocktail shaker, fill it two-thirds of the way with ice, and shake until chilled.

2. Strain over ice into the rocks glass, garnish with the cucumber curl or apple slice, and enjoy.

GREEN GODDESS JUICE: Using a juicer, juice ½ bunch of green kale, 1 large green apple, 1 cucumber, and 2 celery stalks, extracting as much juice as possible. Use immediately or store in the refrigerator.

GLASSWARE: Double rocks glass
GARNISH: Lemon twist

WITCH

Strega is known for its notes of saffron, mint, and juniper, which make it the perfect complement to silver tequila. Fresh lemon juice further heightens the bright yellow color of the amaro, creating a drink that is as visually striking as it is delicious.

1½ oz. silver tequila

¾ oz. Strega

¾ oz. fresh lemon juice

½ oz. Cinnamon Syrup
(see page 109)

1. Place all of the ingredients in a cocktail shaker, fill it two-thirds of the way with ice, and shake until chilled.

2. Double-strain over ice into the double rocks glass, garnish with the lemon twist, and enjoy.

GLASSWARE: Collins glass
GARNISH: Strip of grapefruit peel

TEQUILA MOCKINGBIRD

Eric Passetti and Dennis Leary loved this pun so much, they didn't just name a drink after it—they named their whole bar after it. I've used the word "refreshing" to describe a number of cocktails in this book, but this might be the king of them all. With lime juice, curaçao, elderflower liqueur, and grapefruit juice all present in this delicious mix, each ingredient is more refreshing than the last.

2 oz. silver tequila

1 oz. fresh lime juice

¾ oz. curaçao

¾ oz. elderflower liqueur

½ oz. grapefruit juice

2 dashes of Angostura Bitters

1. Place all of the ingredients in a cocktail shaker, fill it two-thirds of the way with ice, and shake until chilled.

2. Pour the contents of the shaker into the Collins glass, garnish with the strip of grapefruit peel, and enjoy.

GLASSWARE: Mason jar
GARNISH: Orange twist

THE HATCHBACK

You don't see Campari and tequila together as often as you should—Campari's bitterness goes surprisingly well with the rounded, earthy tones of tequila. The bittersweet nature of grapefruit juice makes it a natural complement to the Campari as well, resulting in a brightly colored cocktail that plays its flavors off one another beautifully.

1½ oz. silver tequila

¾ oz. Campari

½ oz. fresh lime juice

½ oz. fresh ruby red grapefruit juice

½ oz. Simple Syrup (see page 40)

Topo Chico, to top

1. Place all of the ingredients, except for the Topo Chico, in a cocktail shaker, fill it two-thirds of the way with ice, and shake until chilled.

2. Strain the cocktail over ice into the mason jar and top with Top Chico.

3. Garnish with the orange twist and enjoy.

GLASSWARE: Coupe
GARNISH: None

RISING SUN

The Rising Sun cocktail gets its name from the maraschino cherry that sits in the bottom of the glass, brightening the cloudy cocktail like the sun coming over the horizon. Tequila and Yellow Chartreuse are a winning combination, and the addition of lime cordial hits with a welcome pop of sweetness.

Salt, for the rim

1 maraschino cherry

1½ oz. silver tequila

⅔ oz. Yellow Chartreuse

½ oz. Rose's Lime Cordial

1 bar spoon sloe gin

1. Wet the rim of the coupe and coat it with salt. Place the cherry in the bottom of the glass and set the rimmed glass aside.

2. Place the tequila, Chartreuse, and cordial in a cocktail shaker, fill it two-thirds of the way with ice, and shake until chilled.

3. Strain into the rimmed glass and top with the sloe gin. Let it filter down through the cocktail and enjoy.

GLASSWARE: Collins glass
GARNISH: Cucumber ribbon

APPLELIZA

With lime, apple, and cucumber flavors floating around this beverage, this is a natural poolside drink, as its bright, summery flavors make it the perfect choice on a hot day.

1⅓ oz. Del Maguey Vida Mezcal

⅓ oz. fresh lime juice

2⅓ oz. apple juice

⅔ oz. Amaro Montenegro

⅓ oz. Cucumber Cordial (see recipe)

1. Chill the Collins glass in the freezer.

2. Fill the chilled glass with ice, add all of the ingredients, and gently stir until chilled.

3. Garnish with the cucumber ribbon and enjoy.

CUCUMBER CORDIAL: Place 1 cucumber peel, ¼ teaspoon Maldon sea salt, 1 cup caster (superfine) sugar, and 2 cups water in a blender and puree until smooth. Strain before using or storing in the refrigerator.

GLASSWARE: Coupe
GARNISH: Maraschino cherry

RED RHUBY

Red Rhuby doubles down on rhubarb flavor, featuring both Aperol and rhubarb liqueur. The result is a cocktail with a slightly tart flavor profile, though the fruity, herbal nature of the peach tea goes a long way toward balancing it out. It's a beautiful, elegant cocktail that is also fairly simple to mix—which makes it the perfect showpiece to trot out for company.

1 oz. tequila

⅔ oz. Aperol

½ oz. Giffard rhubarb liqueur

⅓ oz. dry vermouth

1 oz. iced peach tea

1. Chill the coupe in the freezer.

2. Place all of the ingredients in a mixing glass, fill it two-thirds of the way with ice, and stir until chilled.

3. Strain into the chilled coupe, garnish with the maraschino cherry, and enjoy.

MINESWEEPER FLOWER

The Minesweeper Flower is all about searching for—and finding—floral notes amid this drink's smoky mezcal flavor profile. The grapefruit foam is a lovely topper for this yellow-green cocktail, and adds a beautiful, citrusy aroma that hits the nose and draws you in immediately.

¾ oz. mezcal

¾ oz. Suze

¾ oz. Yellow Chartreuse

Grapefruit Foam
(see recipe), to top

1. Chill the Nick & Nora glass in the refrigerator.

2. Place all of the ingredients, except for the Grapefruit Foam, in a mixing glass, fill it two-thirds of the way with ice, and stir until chilled.

3. Strain into the chilled glass, top with Grapefruit Foam, and enjoy.

   GRAPEFRUIT FOAM: Place ⅔ cup fresh grapefruit juice, 1⅔ oz. Rich Simple Syrup (see page 48), and 1 teaspoon soy lecithin in a blender and puree until the lecithin has dissolved, about 30 seconds. Let the mixture rest for 15 minutes, and then froth it with a milk frother until it is foamy.

GLASSWARE: Nick & Nora glass
GARNISH: None

CAB & MEG

This one feels like the perfect accompaniment to a hearty evening meal. Named for the Cabbage & Nutmeg Shrub, it's a cocktail that manages to be both light and earthy at the same time.

1⅓ oz. mezcal

⅓ oz. dry vermouth

⅓ oz. white crème de cacao

⅔ oz. Cabbage & Nutmeg Shrub (see recipe)

1. Place all of the ingredients in a mixing glass, fill it two-thirds of the way with ice, and stir until chilled.

2. Strain into the Nick & Nora glass and enjoy.

CABBAGE & NUTMEG SHRUB: Place 2 cups chopped cabbage, 1⅔ cups apple cider vinegar, ¼ cup caster (superfine) sugar, ½ cup water, and ½ teaspoon freshly grated nutmeg in a vacuum bag, vacuum seal it, and sous vide at 150ºF for 3 hours. Strain and let the shrub cool before using or storing.

RUM

As it is easily the most diverse spirit on Earth, the process of working with rum while making cocktails is a fun one. But it also can be overwhelming, with offerings from more than 60 countries available to sample.

If you're ever wondering what to select from the dizzying array available, here's a helpful précis: blended rums that have been lightly aged (1 to 4 years) are good go-to's for mixing, and rums in this age range have been rested long enough to let the nature of the spirit come through, but not long enough to take on too much influence from the barrel. That said, there are more than a few instances where a more mature rum, aged from 5 to 14 years, is called for. For those familiar with the higher price tags that extended aging can come with, rest assured—these aged rums, which are also wonderful for sipping neat, carry a much lower price tag than similarly aged Scotches or bourbons. Of course, any trip to the rum section at a liquor store is going to meet with a numbered of flavored rums. In short, the serious practitioner should avoid them at all costs, and take matters into their own hands, either making their own infused version at home, or simply incorporating the flavor they want—coconut, mango, passion fruit—into the cocktail as they mix it.

GLASSWARE: Tiki mug
GARNISH: Edible orchid blossom

THE EXPEDITION

Your home bar might not have the waterfalls and spectacular rum collection of Smuggler's Cove, Martin Cate's world-renowned rum paradise in San Francisco. Luckily, with a few syrups, a blended black rum, and a big ol' tiki mug, you can certainly produce this delightful Cate creation. In the contemporary tiki master's own words: "This drink is called The Expedition, and it's a celebration of the ingredients that Donn Beach, the godfather of tiki, was exposed to and celebrated—coffee and bourbon from New Orleans, fresh citrus from California, and rum and spices from the Caribbean."

2 oz. black blended rum
(such as Coruba, Goslings,
or Hamilton 86)

1 oz. bourbon

¼ oz. Bittermens New
Orleans Coffee Liqueur

1 oz. fresh lime juice

½ oz. Cinnamon Syrup
(see page 109)

½ oz. Honey Syrup
(see page 35)

¼ oz. Vanilla Syrup
(see page 81)

2 oz. seltzer

1. Place all of the ingredients in a cocktail shaker, add crushed ice and 4 to 6 small cubes, and flash mix with a hand blender.

2. Pour the contents of the shaker into the tiki mug.

3. Garnish with the edible orchid blossom and enjoy.

GLASSWARE: Collins glass
GARNISH: 3 pineapple leaves, edible orchid

HURRICANE DROPS

Mixing tropical fruits with gin, ginger, and rum produces a serve that deserves just one adjective: delightful. Spicy, and with a strong backbone, this one is certain to demand your full attention.

1 oz. Plantation 3 Stars Rum

½ oz. gin

¾ oz. fresh lemon juice

1 oz. pineapple juice

1 oz. guava puree

¾ oz. Ginger Syrup (see page 24)

1 bar spoon Herbsaint

4 dashes of Angostura Bitters

1. Place all of the ingredients, except for the bitters, in a mixing glass, add 2 oz. crushed ice, and stir until foamy.

2. Pour the contents of the mixing glass into the Collins glass, add the bitters, and top with more crushed ice.

3. Garnish with the pineapple leaves and edible orchid and enjoy.

GLASSWARE: Tumbler
GARNISH: Fresh Thai basil

SECRET LIFE OF PLANTS

With a name drawn from one of Stevie Wonder's most underrated albums, you can be certain that every element of this cocktail is in harmony. That concord is largely owed to the Mango & Oolong Syrup, which supplies bright and toasty tones.

1½ oz. lightly aged rum

¾ oz. Mango & Oolong Syrup (see recipe)

¾ oz. fresh lime juice

¼ oz. Orgeat (see page 30)

¼ oz. falernum

10 drops of 10 Percent Saline Solution (see page 35)

Dash of absinthe

1. Place all of the ingredients in a cocktail shaker, fill it two-thirds of the way with ice, and shake until chilled.

2. Fill the tumbler with crushed ice and strain the cocktail over it.

3. Top with more crushed ice, garnish with the fresh Thai basil, and enjoy.

MANGO & OOLONG SYRUP: Place ¾ cup water in a saucepan and heat it to 195°F. Add ¼ cup loose-leaf oolong tea and steep for 5 minutes. Strain the tea, discard the leaves, and return the tea to the saucepan. Add 30 oz. mango puree, 30 oz. sugar, 1 (12 oz.) can of mango nectar, and a scant 2½ teaspoons citric acid and warm the mixture over low heat, stirring to dissolve the sugar. When the syrup is well combined, remove the pan from heat and let it cool completely before using or storing.

GLASSWARE: Collins glass
GARNISH: Cacao nibs, star anise pod

DAUPHIN

Presentation is a major piece of The Dauphin, as the bowl full of pebble ice is supposed to elicit feelings of grandeur and riches. But that decadent vibe is not just for show—the flavor, which bounces between molasses, chocolate, chiles, anise, and coconut—will bring to mind the dessert menu at a three-star restaurant.

1½ oz. Goslings Black Seal Rum

2 dashes of Miracle Mile Bitters Co. Chocolate Chili Bitters

½ oz. Demerara Syrup (see page 20)

½ oz. Ancho Reyes

1 oz. absinthe

1¼ oz. toasted coconut almond milk

1. Place the Collins glass in a bowl and build the cocktail in the glass, adding the ingredients in the order they are listed.

2. Fill the bowl and the glass with pebble ice and stir the cocktail until it is chilled and combined.

3. Garnish with the cacao nibs and star anise and enjoy.

GLASSWARE: Collins glass
GARNISH: Yellow viola blossom

SUN BREAKING THROUGH THE FOG

Ten to One rum has a peppery, lemongrass quality that makes it the perfect complement to the pineapple, port, and amaro. The Sun Breaking through the Fog is a beautiful blend of subtle flavors—everything in the glass is there for a reason, adding a unique quality to every sip.

¾ oz. Ten to One Caribbean Dark Rum

¾ oz. Fonseca 10-Year Tawny Port

¾ oz. Amaro Montenegro

¾ oz. fresh lime juice

¾ oz. Pineapple Syrup (see recipe)

1. Place all of the ingredients in a cocktail shaker, fill it two-thirds of the way with ice, and shake until chilled.

2. Fill the Collins glass with crushed ice and strain the cocktail over it.

3. Garnish with the yellow viola blossom and enjoy.

    PINEAPPLE SYRUP: Combine equal parts pineapple juice and sugar in a blender and blend on high for 2 minutes. Let the syrup settle, then transfer it to a container and chill in the refrigerator until ready to use.

GLASSWARE: Coupe
GARNISH: Ribbon, sprig of fresh lavender

DARKNESS & DISGRACE

There are elements of an Espresso Martini here, but the Darkness & Disgrace cocktail doesn't overcommit to coffee flavor, instead tempering that element with port. The result is something a little fruity and a little bitter—an unusual combination, but one that really seems to work. Of course, the elephant in the room is the inclusion of egg yolk, but this too works surprisingly well, adding a bit of richness and body to the drink.

1¾ oz. Diplomático Reserva Exclusiva Rum

¾ oz. Quinta do Noval Port

2 teaspoons Bepe Tosolini Exprè Coffee Liqueur

2 teaspoons Simple Syrup (see page 40)

1 egg yolk

1. Place all of the ingredients in a cocktail shaker, fill it two-thirds of the way with ice, and shake until chilled.

2. Strain into the coupe, use the ribbon to affix the sprig of fresh lavender to the stem of the glass, and enjoy.

GLASSWARE: Rocks glass
GARNISH: Passion fruit slice, fresh mint

RUM BA BA

Cocktails are often praised for being "light" and "effervescent," but how about something rich and creamy, instead? The Rum Ba Ba combines rum, heavy cream, and Orgeat with lemon juice, passion fruit, and bitters to create a cocktail that touches all corners of the flavor spectrum. It's a sweeter drink, and it's certainly on the heavy side—which makes sense, given that it takes its name from France's famously sticky cake.

1½ oz. Appleton Estate Reserve Blend Rum

1½ oz. heavy cream

1 oz. Orgeat (see page 30)

½ oz. fresh lemon juice

1¼ oz. passion fruit puree

2 dashes of Peychaud's Bitters

1. Place all of the ingredients in a cocktail shaker, fill it two-thirds of the way with ice, and shake until chilled.

2. Fill a rocks glass with ice and double-strain the cocktail over it.

3. Garnish with the passion fruit slice and fresh mint and enjoy.

GLASSWARE: Rocks glass
GARNISH: Fresh mint, orange slice, maraschino cherry

MAI KINDA GAI

A take on the classic Mai Tai, Mai Kinda Gai utilizes a very specific ingredient: Banana & Cashew Orgeat. The nutty, banana flavor adds something special to an already flavorful drink, transporting you to a tropical paradise with every sip.

¾ oz. Banana & Cashew Orgeat (see recipe)

1½ oz. Hamilton Guyana 86 Rum

½ oz. Mandarine Napoléon

1 oz. fresh lime juice

½ oz. Ron Zacapa 23 Rum, to float

1. Place all of the ingredients, except for the Ron Zacapa, in a cocktail shaker, fill it two-thirds of the way with ice, and shake until chilled.

2. Fill the rocks glass with ice and strain the cocktail over it.

3. Float the Ron Zacapa on top of the drink, pouring it slowly over the back of a spoon.

4. Garnish with the fresh mint, orange slice, and maraschino cherry and enjoy.

BANANA & CASHEW ORGEAT: In a saucepan, bring 1 cup of cashew milk to a simmer. Place 2 cups of sugar in a container, pour the warmed milk over it, and stir until the sugar has dissolved. Let the mixture cool completely and then stir in 4 oz. of Giffard Banane Du Brésil. Use immediately or store in the refrigerator.

GLASSWARE: Coupe
GARNISH: Lime wheel

LYCHEE DAIQUIRI

Lychee is quickly becoming a cocktail staple, and this Daiquiri iteration will clue you in as to why. This is on the sweeter side for a Daiquiri, but the Jamaican Bitters help tamp down the sweetness ever so slightly, ensuring that the flavors in this delicious concoction remain perfectly in balance.

2 oz. unaged rum

2 dashes of Bittercube Jamaican No. 2 Bitters

1 oz. fresh lime juice

¾ oz. Lychee Syrup (see recipe)

1. Place all of the ingredients in a cocktail shaker, fill it two-thirds of the way with ice, and shake until chilled.

2. Strain into the coupe, garnish with the lime wheel, and enjoy.

   LYCHEE SYRUP: Remove the skins and seeds from ½ lb. of lychees, place them in a blender, and puree until smooth. Pour the puree into a saucepan, add 1 cup sugar and 1 cup water, and cook over medium heat, stirring to dissolve the sugar. Cook until the desired consistency is achieved. Remove the pan from heat and let the syrup cool completely. Strain before using or storing in the refrigerator.

GLASSWARE: Nick & Nora glass
GARNISH: Fresh rosemary

THE BANKS SOUR

The Banks Sour is a complex cocktail, but every little component is there for a reason. Ingredients like Coconut-Washed Rum, Dry Spice Syrup, Sage & Rosemary Tincture, and Cherry & Cider Foam are unusual, to be sure—but they combine to create something spectacular. The subtle spices, herbs, and floral notes play throughout the cocktail, and the sour bite from the lime juice brings everything together in the best possible way.

1½ oz. Coconut-Washed Rum (see recipe)

¾ oz. fresh lime juice

½ oz. Dry Spice Syrup (see recipe)

5 drops of Sage & Rosemary Tincture (see recipe)

½ oz. cava

Cherry & Cider Foam, to top (see recipe)

1. Chill the Nick & Nora glass in the freezer.

2. Place the rum, lime juice, syrup, and tincture in a cocktail shaker, fill it two-thirds of the way with ice, and shake until chilled.

3. Add the cava to the shaker and double-strain the cocktail into the chilled glass.

4. Layer the foam on top of the drink, garnish with the fresh rosemary, and enjoy.

COCONUT-WASHED RUM: In a large bowl, combine ½ cup unrefined coconut oil with a 750 ml bottle of Banks 7 Golden Age Rum. Stir until well combined and place the rum in the freezer overnight. Remove the hardened layer of fat, strain the rum through a coffee filter, and use as desired.

DRY SPICE SYRUP: In a saucepan, bring 2 cups of water to a boil and add 3 cinnamon sticks, 3 whole cloves, and 1 star anise pod. Remove from heat and cover the pan for 3 minutes. Add 3 cups sugar, stir to dissolve, and let the syrup cool completely. Strain before using or storing.

SAGE & ROSEMARY TINCTURE: Add the leaves from 5 sprigs of sage and 5 sprigs of rosemary to 1 cup vodka. Let the mixture steep for 3 days and strain before using or storing.

CHERRY & CIDER FOAM: In a saucepan, combine 3 cups pitted cherries and 12 oz. Crispin Rosé Cider and simmer over low heat for 20 minutes. Strain and let the liquid cool completely. Add 1 teaspoon Versawhip and place the mixture in a charged whipping gun..

GLASSWARE: Rocks glass
GARNISH: Torched orange peel (see page 129), coffee beans

THE PROJECT

When you order a rum cocktail, you can't help but expect it to be sweet. The Project turns that expectation on its head, incorporating Coffee Syrup to add a bitter, earthy element to the cocktail alongside the floral and herbal notes of Cynar and Aperol. There's a lot going on here, and it works surprisingly well.

2 oz. Santa Teresa 1796 rum

¼ oz. Cynar

1 oz. Aperol

¼ oz. Coffee Syrup
(see recipe)

1. Place all of the ingredients in a cocktail shaker, fill it two-thirds of the way with ice, and shake until chilled.

2. Double-strain over an ice sphere into the rocks glass, garnish with the torched orange peel and coffee beans, and enjoy.

   COFFEE SYRUP: Place equal parts water and sugar in a saucepan and add coffee beans, using 10 beans per quart of water. Bring to a boil, remove the pan from heat, and the mixture steep for 4 hours. Strain before using or storing in the refrigerator.

GLASSWARE: Double rocks glass
GARNISH: Pineapple leaf, edible orchid

SECRET OF THE LOST LAGOON

If you like tiki drinks, this is exactly what you're looking for: a mix of light and dark rum, a variety of fresh fruit juices and syrups, and . . . coffee? Yes, that's right—this cocktail includes a splash of cold brew, which introduces a surprisingly welcome bitter element to an otherwise sweet cocktail.

1½ oz. Coruba Dark Rum

½ oz. Wray & Nephew Overproof Rum

¾ oz. fresh lime juice

½ oz. pineapple juice

½ oz. cold-brew coffee

½ oz. Ginger Syrup (see page 24)

¾ oz. Vanilla Syrup (see page 81)

1. Place all of the ingredients in a cocktail shaker, fill it halfway with crushed ice, and shake until chilled.

2. Pour the contents of the shaker into the double rocks glass, garnish with the pineapple leaf and edible orchid, and enjoy.

GLASSWARE: Rocks glass
GARNISH: None

PEDRO MARTINEZ COCKTAIL

A rum-based take on a cocktail traditionally made with gin, this serve features a wide range of ingredients including absinthe, maraschino liqueur, and a combined 13 dashes of two different types of bitters. All that complexity serves a purpose, though—and that purpose is to create an absolutely delicious cocktail. It takes a confident mixologist to dream up something as complex as the Pedro Martinez Cocktail, but it drinks as smooth as the legend's windup.

1 small strip of lime peel

2 oz. demerara rum

1 oz. Cocchi Vermouth di Torino

¼ oz. maraschino liqueur

10 drops of Angostura Bitters

3 dashes of orange bitters

4 drops of absinthe

2 strips of lemon peel

1. Express the strip of lime peel over a mixing glass and then drop the peel into the glass.

2. Add ice and all of the remaining ingredients, except for the strips of lemon peel, and stir until chilled.

3. Strain over a large ice cube into the rocks glass, express the strips of lemon peel over the drink, discard them, and enjoy.

GLASSWARE: Collins glass
GARNISH: 1 teaspoon shaved fresh ginger

THE POWER OF ONE

Coconut milk is an underutilized cocktail ingredient—when used appropriately, it can bring a rich, velvety texture that transforms an otherwise mundane cocktail into something extraordinary. But there's nothing mundane about the Power of One, and the addition of coconut milk takes what was already a delicious mix of flavors over the top.

2 oz. Appleton Estate
Reserve Blend Rum

1 oz. coconut milk

1 oz. fresh lime juice

1 oz. Demerara Syrup
(see page 20)

1. Place all of the ingredients in a cocktail shaker, fill it two-thirds of the way with ice, and shake until chilled.

2. Fill the Collins glass with crushed ice and strain the cocktail over it.

3. Top with more crushed ice, garnish with the shaved ginger, and enjoy.

GLASSWARE: Collins glass
GARNISH: Lemongrass stalk

LEMONGRASS MOJITO

There's nothing quite as refreshing as a Mojito, and the Lemongrass Mojito adds lemongrass tea and apple juice to the mix—just enough to give the drink a rosy hue and impart a new, subtle layer of flavor. It's a drink that goes down easy (maybe even easier than a classic Mojito), and is the perfect thing to reach for on a hot summer day.

2 teaspoons loose-leaf lemongrass tea

6 fresh mint leaves

1¾ oz. rum (white or dark)

¾ oz. Simple Syrup (see page 40)

¾ oz. apple juice

¾ oz. fresh lime juice

1⅜ oz. seltzer, to top

1. Place the loose-leaf tea in 1½ oz. of hot water and steep for 4 minutes.

2. Add the mint leaves to the Collins glass and muddle. Strain the tea into the glass, add the rum, syrup, apple juice, and lime juice, and stir until the mixture is at room temperature.

3. Add ice and top with the seltzer.

4. Garnish with the lemongrass stalk and enjoy.

GLASSWARE: Cocktail glass
GARNISH: Trimmed banana leaves, edible flower

KAGANO

If you're not familiar with umesu, it's the vinegar-like juice produced by salt-packed ume plums. You probably wouldn't want to drink it on its own, but it makes a fantastic addition to this rum-based cocktail. The Kagano is experimenting with a lot of unusual flavors (how often do you see Scotch and banana liqueur in the same drink?), which, to me, is what makes it a must-try cocktail.

1½ oz. Bacardi Reserva Ocho Rum

½ oz. umesu

½ oz. blended Scotch whisky

¼ oz. banana liqueur

Dash of 10 Percent Saline Solution (see page 35)

1 strip of orange peel

1. Place all of the ingredients, except for the strip of orange peel, in a mixing glass, fill it two-thirds of the way with ice, and stir until chilled.

2. Strain into the cocktail glass, express the strip of orange peel over the drink, and discard the orange peel.

3. Garnish with the banana leaves and edible flower and enjoy.

GLASSWARE: Shot glasses
GARNISH: None

THE FRUIT STAND

How about a shot? A good cocktail book needs at least one inventive shot, and the The Fruit Stand is a creative (and surprisingly flavorful) one. The mix of rum, apricot, pineapple, and lime flavors ensure that this shooter goes down incredibly smooth, making it a good option even for those who don't usually love taking shots.

1½ oz. Plantation Stiggins Fancy Pineapple Rum

½ oz. Giffard Abricot du Roussillon

1 oz. pineapple juice

½ oz. fresh lime juice

¼ oz. Simple Syrup (see page 40)

4 dashes of Peychaud's Bitters, to top

1. Place all of the ingredients, except for the bitters, in a cocktail shaker, fill it two-thirds of the way with ice, and shake until chilled.

2. Double-strain into 2 shot glasses, top each shot with the bitters, and enjoy.

GLASSWARE: Coupe
GARNISH: Edible flower

AOSHIMA ISLAND

Plum wine is a wonderful ingredient that isn't used in nearly enough cocktails—at least not in the United States. Popular in Japan, it has a sweet and tangy flavor profile that makes it the perfect addition to a wide range of cocktails. In this case, it pairs perfectly with rum and ginger, resulting in a flavorful cocktail that will light up your taste buds without overwhelming them.

1 oz. light rum

1 oz. plum wine

1 oz. ginger liqueur

½ oz. Orgeat (see page 30)

½ oz fresh lemon juice

3 dashes of Peychaud's Bitters

1. Chill the coupe in the freezer.

2. Place all of the ingredients in a cocktail shaker, fill it two-thirds of the way with ice, and shake until chilled.

3. Strain into the chilled coupe, garnish with the edible flower, and enjoy.

GLASSWARE: Nick & Nora glass
GARNISH: Fresh sage leaf

BURNT SAGE SOUR

Sour and spice pair well together, and a cocktail that can balance those two competing flavors is guaranteed a winner in my book. Enter the Burnt Sage Sour, which takes overproof spiced rum and chile liqueur and pits them against pineapple juice, lime juice, and sage to create a sour cocktail with a considerable kick.

1 oz. Plantation O.F.T.D. Rum

1 oz. Ancho Reyes

1 oz. pineapple juice

½ oz. fresh lime juice

1 oz. Burnt Sugar Syrup (see recipe)

2 fresh sage leaves

1. Place all of the ingredients in a cocktail shaker, fill it two-thirds of the way with ice, and shake until chilled.

2. Double-strain into the Nick & Nora glass. Lightly brûlée the additional fresh sage leaf with a torch, garnish the cocktail with it, and enjoy.

BURNT SUGAR SYRUP: Place 1 cup brown sugar in a saucepan and cook it over low heat, swirling the pan occasionally, until the sugar has melted. Cook for another minute and remove the pan from heat. Slowly and very carefully, since the mixture is likely going to spatter, pour in 1 cup boiling water, stirring continually. Return the pan to the stove and cook over medium heat for 2 minutes. Remove the pan from heat and let the syrup cool completely before using or storing in the refrigerator.

GLASSWARE: Rocks glass
GARNISH: Fresh mint

THE RATTLE AND THE RHYTHM

The inclusion of jicama juice and smoked sea salt takes this cocktail into the stratosphere. Coffee bitters, too, add a unique element to this serve.

1½ oz. Hamilton Jamaica Gold Rum

¾ oz. fresh lime juice

¾ oz. Demerara Syrup (see page 20)

¾ oz. freshly pressed jicama juice

4 fresh mint leaves

Pinch of smoked sea salt

2 dashes of coffee bitters

1. Place all of the ingredients in a cocktail shaker, fill it two-thirds of the way with ice, and shake until chilled.

2. Fill the rocks glass with crushed ice and strain the cocktail over it.

3. Garnish the cocktail with the fresh mint and enjoy.

GLASSWARE: Cocktail glass
GARNISH: None

POLAR SHORTCUT

Originally created to celebrate the opening of a new airline route between Copenhagen and Tokyo, the original Polar Shortcut blended dark rum, Cointreau, cherry brandy, and dry vermouth in equal measure to create a beautiful blend of strong, assertive flavors. This version foregrounds the rum and pulls the Cointreau and cherry brandy into the deep background to serve as complementary rather than competing flavors. It's a wonderful spin on an old classic.

1⅓ oz. aged rum

2 bar spoons Cointreau

2 bar spoons cherry brandy

⅔ oz. dry vermouth

1. Place all of the ingredients in a mixing glass, fill it two-thirds of the way with ice, and stir until chilled.

2. Strain into the cocktail glass and enjoy.

GLASSWARE: Rocks glass
GARNISH: None

DOT LINE

Remember the Indiana Jones movies? How whenever Indy would travel to a new location, you'd see a dotted line crawling its way across a map? Well, that's the spirit in which this cocktail was created. Dot Line features ingredients from eight countries and four continents, making it a truly international experience.

¼ oz. ground Kenyan coffee

1 ⅓ oz. Bacardi Carta Blanca Rum

⅔ oz. umeshu

1 bar spoon Pedro Ximénez sherry

1 bar spoon St-Germain

Dash of balsamic vinegar

1. Place a coffee dripper over a mixing glass, line the coffee dripper with a filter, and place the coffee in the filter.

2. Pour the rum, umeshu, sherry, and St-Germain over the coffee and let them drip into the glass.

3. Add the balsamic vinegar to the mixing glass, then ice, and stir to incorporate.

4. Strain over an ice sphere into the rocks glass and enjoy.

GLASSWARE: Champagne flute
GARNISH: Strip of lemon peel

I WISH I WAS IN NEW ORLEANS

I Wish I Was in New Orleans is a twist on the French 75—one that prominently features both rum and elderflower liqueur. It certainly changes the flavor profile of the cocktail, but the result is no less elegant than the original.

⅔ oz. Havana Club 7 Year Rum

⅓ oz. Giffard wild elderflower liqueur

1¼ teaspoons fresh lime juice

2 dashes of Peychaud's Bitters

Brut Champagne, to top

1. Place all of the ingredients, except for the Champagne, in a cocktail shaker, fill it two-thirds of the way with ice, and shake vigorously until chilled.

2. Strain the cocktail into the Champagne flute and top with Champagne.

3. Garnish with the strip of lemon peel and enjoy.

GLASSWARE: Rocks glass
GARNISH: 2 Griottines

ZACAPA MARTINI

Here's a question: How far can you stray from the original Martini recipe while still calling a cocktail a Martini? Apparently, the answer is quite far. The Zacapa Martini is simple: rum with a splash of bourbon. That simplicity certainly honors the spirit of the Martini, and while the flavor of the cocktail is obviously very different, the idea of accenting one strong flavor with a subtle splash of another is very Martini-like.

2 oz. Ron Zacapa 23 Rum

1 bar spoon Bulleit Bourbon

1. Place the rum and bourbon in a mixing glass, fill it two-thirds of the way with ice, and stir until chilled.

2. Strain into the rocks glass, garnish with the Griottines, and enjoy.

VODKA

Vodka's lack of a distinctive flavor allows it to find a comfortable place beside a stunning amount of other ingredients, making it a perfect spirit for cocktails. You can pair it with damn near anything, as evidenced by its presence in a diverse group of cocktails that spans from Martinis to Bloody Marys and White Russians. It plays well with many other spirits and complements whatever it is added to, which is not something you can say about other types of alcohol. This ease puts many in the craft cocktail space off, to the point that they refuse to work with vodka. But, as you know, in the contemporary cocktail world, a hardline stance is simply the progenitor of considerable opportunities. As you'll see, a number of mixologists have seized upon them, filling the substantial open space with unusual ingredients and innovative blends that will delight vodka enthusiasts, and win over those who are skeptical of the spirit.

GLASSWARE: Coupe
GARNISH: Fresh mint

AMELIA

Purple conjures images of romance, a quality that is fitting for the Amelia. Centered around the Blackberry Puree that provides the eye-catching color and sweet-and-sour profile, it's a drink to share with someone special.

1½ oz. vodka

1 oz. Blackberry Puree
(see recipe)

¾ oz. St-Germain

½ oz. fresh lemon juice

1. Chill the coupe in the freezer.

2. Place all of the ingredients in a cocktail shaker, fill it two-thirds of the way with ice, and shake until chilled.

3. Strain the cocktail into the chilled coupe, garnish with fresh mint, and enjoy.

   BLACKBERRY PUREE: Place ¼ lb. fresh or thawed frozen blackberries, 2 tablespoons caster (superfine) sugar, 2 tablespoons water, and 2 tablespoons fresh lemon juice in a blender and puree until smooth. Strain before using or storing.

GLASSWARE: Coupe
GARNISH: 3 raspberries

LEAVE IT TO ME

A riff on the classic Clover Club cocktail that swaps out the gin for vodka, the Leave It to Me is keyed by the Lazzaroni Maraschino, which is slightly bitter and not quite as funky as the much more commonly used Luxardo.

2 oz. Grey Goose Vodka

¼ oz. Lazzaroni Maraschino Liqueur

¾ oz. Raspberry Syrup (see page 156)

¾ oz. fresh lemon juice

1 oz. egg white

1. Place all of the ingredients in a cocktail shaker and dry shake for 15 seconds.

2. Add ice and shake until chilled.

3. Double-strain the cocktail into the coupe, garnish with the raspberries, and enjoy.

GLASSWARE: Coupe
GARNISH: None

ROOT HEALER

One thing that is often overlooked by home bartenders is how powerful rimming a glass can be as a tool. The Root Healer is a good example of this—with the accents of salt and smoke, each of its many components comes to life.

Smoked salt, for the rim

1½ oz. pear vodka

¼ oz. Calvados VSOP

¼ oz. Asian pear puree

1 oz. tamarind nectar

¼ oz. Passion Fruit Syrup
(see page 48)

¼ oz. fresh lime juice

2 fresh shiso leaves

½ oz. Simple Syrup
(see page 40)

1. Wet the rim of the coupe and coat it with smoked salt.

2. Add all of the remaining ingredients to a cocktail shaker, fill it two-thirds of the way with ice, and shake until chilled.

3. Double-strain the cocktail into the coupe and enjoy.

GLASSWARE: Collins glass
GARNISH: Matcha, pumpkin-and-mint bouquet, lime wheel, edible flower

SHINJUKU GARDENS

Midori's bright green hue, and its time as a key ingredient in a number of re-grettable drinks mixed up during the 1980s—aka the nadir of craft cocktails—means that many have negative associations with it. However, that stance is due for some revision, as Suntory introduced a revised formula for the spirit in 2012. Now featuring two Japanese melon varieties and a drier profile, Midori is ready for a renaissance.

Sugar, for the rim

2 cucumber slices

2 oz. Beluga Noble Vodka

½ oz. Midori

½ oz. Luxardo maraschino liqueur

¾ oz. fresh lemon juice

½ oz. Simple Syrup (see page 40)

Fever-Tree Sparkling Lime & Yuzu Tonic Water, to top

1. Wet the rim of the Collins glass and coat it with sugar. Add ice to the rimmed glass.

2. Place all of the remaining ingredients, except the tonic water, in a cocktail shaker and muddle.

3. Add ice and shake until chilled.

4. Strain the cocktail into the rimmed glass and top with tonic water.

5. Garnish with the matcha, bouquet, lime wheel, and edible flower and enjoy.

SMOKED RASAM: Dice 15 tomatoes, place them in a saucepan, and cook over medium heat for about 20 minutes. Add coriander seeds, curry leaves, and mustard seeds to taste, and the Masala Water (see recipe), stir to combine, and remove the pan from heat. Place the saucepan in a large roasting pan. Place hickory wood chips in a ramekin, coat a strip of paper towel with canola oil, and insert it in the center of the wood chips. Set the ramekin in the roasting pan, carefully light the wick, and wait until the wood chips ignite. Cover the roasting pan with aluminum foil and smoke the rasam for 1 hour.

MASALA WATER: Place 2 oz. dried mango in a bowl of hot water and soak it for 30 minutes. Place the rehydrated mango, 3 oz. cilantro, 3 green chile peppers, ½ teaspoon black pepper, ¼ teaspoon grated fresh ginger, and 2 teaspoons dried mint in a food processor and blitz until the mixture is a smooth paste. Stir the paste into 4 cups water and use as desired.

GLASSWARE: Rocks glass
GARNISH: Fried curry leaf

WHISTLEPODU

Rasam, a spicy-and-sour tomato soup popular in southern Indian cuisine, provides the inspiration for this ingenious twist on the Bloody Mary. As brilliant on the palate as it is to the eye, the Whistlepodu is certain to elicit cheers from the entire crowd at your next brunch.

2 oz. Smoked Rasam (see recipe)

2 oz. vodka

¾ oz. honey

¾ oz. fresh lime juice

1 oz. club soda

1. Place all of the ingredients in a mixing glass, stir to combine, and then carbonate the cocktail.

2. Pour the cocktail over ice into the rocks glass, garnish with the fried curry leaf, and enjoy.

GLASSWARE: Coupe
GARNISH: None

EAST OF EDEN

Ever wondered what the Piña Colada would be if you pulled it off of the cruise ship and dressed it up in California chic? The East of Eden is your answer, taking those familiar tropical flavors and effortlessly transforming them into something elegant.

1½ oz. vodka

½ oz. coconut rum

¼ oz. heavy cream

½ oz. egg white

½ oz. fresh lemon juice

½ oz. Simple Syrup
(see page 40)

2 dashes of lavender bitters

1. Place all of the ingredients in a cocktail shaker, fill it two-thirds of the way with ice, and shake until chilled.

2. Strain into the coupe and enjoy.

GLASSWARE: Cocktail glass
GARNISH: Edible pink glitter

ZIGGY STARDUST

If you prefer cocktails with a sour flavor profile, it's hard to imagine a better cocktail than the Ziggy Stardust. Lemon juice and Lemon-Infused Vodka are balanced perfectly with pomegranate juice and crème de cassis, topped with a lovely egg white foam. Of course, what makes the drink truly visually arresting is the garnish of edible glitter in the shape of the iconic *Aladdin Sane* lightning bolt. It's a drink that honors David Bowie's legacy in the most delicious possible way.

1¾ oz. Lemon-Infused Vodka (see recipe)

2 teaspoons crème de cassis

1¾ oz. pomegranate juice

½ oz. fresh lemon juice

1 egg white

1. Place all of the ingredients in a cocktail shaker and dry shake for 15 seconds.

2. Add ice and shake until chilled.

3. Strain into the cocktail glass.

4. Garnish with edible pink glitter, in the shape of the iconic *Aladdin Sane* lightning bolt.

   LEMON-INFUSED VODKA: Peel 1 lemon, place the peel in a mason jar filled with vodka (or directly in the bottle of vodka), and let steep for 24 to 36 hours. Strain before using or storing.

GLASSWARE: Copper cup
GARNISH: Pineapple leaf, dehydrated lime wheel

WYNWOOD MULE

The Wynwood Mule adds Smoked Pineapple Syrup to the vodka, lime juice, and ginger beer usually found in a Mule-style cocktail, a bold and delicious choice that takes a classic cocktail into a new realm.

1½ oz. vodka

1 oz. fresh lime juice

¾ oz. Smoked Pineapple Syrup (see recipe)

2 oz. ginger beer

1. Place all of the ingredients in the copper cup, fill it with crushed ice, and gently stir.

2. Garnish with the pineapple leaf and dehydrated lime wheel and enjoy.

SMOKED PINEAPPLE SYRUP: Place 4 to 6 whole pineapples in a smoker, set it to 220°F, and smoke the pineapples until they are charred, 3 to 4 hours. Remove from the smoker and let them cool. Chop the pineapples, making sure to reserve any juices, and weigh them. Place the pineapples and any juices in a saucepan and add 60 percent of their weight in water. Bring to a rolling boil and cook for 15 minutes. Stir in 40 percent of the pineapples' weight in sugar and simmer for 45 minutes. Place the mixture in a food processor and blitz until pureed. Strain the syrup and let it cool completely before using or storing. If you're looking for a quicker way to get a smoky flavor into pineapple, slice the pineapples and cook them on a charcoal grill for 15 minutes. Remove them from the grill and follow the same method recommended above.

GLASSWARE: Collins glass
GARNISH: Fresh mint

THE HALLIWELL

There's something lovely about a light, fruity cocktail, and the Halliwell certainly has plenty of love to go around. Fresh lemon juice and strawberry puree add delicious, fruity elements to the cocktail, while the inclusion of Cocchi Americano Rosa adds a slightly herbaceous note that keeps the drink from being too sweet. And of course, the Ginger Syrup and mint leaves add flavorful and aromatic components of their own.

1½ oz. Stoli vodka

½ oz. Cocchi Americano Rosa

1 oz. Ginger Syrup (see page 24)

1 oz. fresh lemon juice

1 oz. strawberry puree

8 fresh mint leaves

1. Place all of the ingredients in a cocktail shaker, fill it two-thirds of the way with ice, and shake until chilled.

2. Double-strain over ice into the Collins glass, garnish with additional fresh mint, and enjoy.

GLASSWARE: Copper cup
GARNISH: Slice of fresh ginger, edible orchid blossom

COPPER CUP #4

A refreshingly simple mix of complementary flavors. The subtle floral notes of elderflower liqueur and Hibiscus Syrup add just a little something extra to the ginger and lime, taking an otherwise straightforward recipe and elevating it into a bona fide high-society cocktail.

2 oz. Absolut Elyx Vodka

¾ oz. St-Germain

¼ oz. freshly pressed ginger juice

¾ oz. fresh lemon juice

¼ oz. Hibiscus Syrup (see recipe)

1. Place all of the ingredients in a cocktail shaker, fill it two-thirds of the way with ice, and shake vigorously until chilled.

2. Fill the copper cup with crushed ice, strain the cocktail over it, and top with more crushed ice.

3. Garnish with the slice of ginger and orchid blossom and enjoy.

   HIBISCUS SYRUP: Place 1 teaspoon loose-leaf hibiscus tea in 1 cup Simple Syrup (see page 40) and steep for 10 days. Strain before using or storing in the refrigerator.

GLASSWARE: Pint glass
GARNISH: Blackberry, fresh mint

BLACKBIRD

The combination of sweet tea vodka and blackberry puree makes for a cocktail on the sweeter side of the spectrum, but the addition of lemon juice adds just enough tartness to balance out the sugar and keep this serve firmly in deliciously drinkable territory.

2 oz. sweet tea vodka

½ oz. blackberry puree

¾ oz. fresh lemon juice

¾ oz. Simple Syrup
(see page 40)

1. Place all of the ingredients in a cocktail shaker, fill it two-thirds of the way with ice, and shake until chilled.

2. Strain over pebble ice into the pint glass, garnish with the blackberry and fresh mint, and enjoy.

GLASSWARE: Collins glass
GARNISH: Sugar-coated blueberries

POLAR VORTEX

Instead of buying flavored vodka, it's always worth seeing if you can do better with a version that you infused at home. The Polar Vortex is a good example of what is possible if you take matters into your own hands.

2 oz. Blueberry Tea–Infused Vodka (see recipe)

½ oz. Lavender Syrup (see recipe)

Cream soda, to top

1 oz. cream of coconut

1. Fill the Collins glass with ice, add the vodka and syrup, and stir until chilled.

2. Top with cream soda and layer the cream of coconut on top of the cocktail by pouring it slowly over the back of a spoon.

3. Garnish with sugar-coated blueberries and enjoy.

BLUEBERRY TEA–INFUSED VODKA: Place 2 bags of blueberry tea and a 750 ml bottle of vodka in a large mason jar and steep for 4 hours. Remove the tea bags and use immediately or store.

LAVENDER SYRUP: Combine 250 grams sugar, 250 milliliters water, and 1.25 grams dried lavender in a saucepan and bring the mixture to a boil over medium heat, stirring to dissolve the sugar. Remove the pan from heat, let the syrup cool completely, and strain before using or storing.

GLASSWARE: Cocktail glass
GARNISH: Fresh cilantro

SACSAYHUAMAN

With only two ingredients, you could be forgiven for assuming that this cocktail is straightforward, but the Passion Fruit Mix carries a surprising depth of flavor, and will tantalize your palate with every sip. The Pepper Vodka adds some serious heat that complements the sweet-tart passion fruit, resulting in a cocktail that boldly dances across your tongue.

1½ oz. Pepper Vodka (see recipe)

2 oz. Passion Fruit Mix (see recipe)

1. Place the ingredients in a cocktail shaker, fill it two-thirds of the way with ice, and shake until chilled.

2. Strain into the cocktail glass, garnish with fresh cilantro, and enjoy.

   PEPPER VODKA: Place 6 habanero chile peppers in a jar, fill the jar with vodka, and store in a cool, dry place for about a week. Strain before using or storing at room temperature.

   PASSION FRUIT MIX: Place 1½ cups passion fruit puree and 1 cup Rich Simple Syrup (see page 48) in a blender and puree until combined. Use immediately or store in the refrigerator.

GLASSWARE: Cocktail glass
GARNISH: None

POMEGRANATE COSMO

What cocktail book would be complete without a Cosmopolitan recipe? This thoughtful take on the classic recipe incorporates pomegranate liqueur and pomegranate juice in place of the traditional cranberry juice, giving the drink a deep red coloration that looks absolutely beautiful in a cocktail glass.

1½ oz. vodka

½ oz. Pama Pomegranate Liqueur

½ oz. Pierre Ferrand Dry Curaçao

½ oz. fresh lime juice

½ oz. pomegranate juice

1. Place all of the ingredients in a cocktail shaker, fill it two-thirds of the way with ice, and shake until chilled.

2. Strain into the cocktail glass and enjoy.

GLASSWARE: Coupe
GARNISH: Slice of English cucumber

PORTLAND PERESTROIKA

What elevates this cocktail is the inclusion of a splash of pear nectar, which adds a fruity element that is still subtle enough to not overwhelm the palate. Otherwise, this mixture of vodka, sugar, cucumber, and lime is much in line with what you'd expect—one that plays with classic flavors and avoids the temptation to get too fancy. It's the rare cocktail that works just as well as a brunch sipper as it does as a nightcap.

1 lime wedge

Dash of caster (superfine) sugar

2 slices of English cucumber

2 oz. Lovejoy Vodka

½ oz. pear nectar

1. Place the lime wedge and sugar in a cocktail shaker and muddle.

2. Add ice and the remaining ingredients and shake until chilled.

3. Strain into the coupe, garnish with additional slice of cucumber, and enjoy.

GLASSWARE: Rocks glass
GARNISH: Grapefruit wheel

ITALIAN GREYHOUND

While a Greyhound cocktail is traditionally made with grapefruit juice and vodka or gin, the Italian Greyhound introduces a pair of Italy-inclined ingredients that elevate this drink into something much more refined.

1 oz. vodka

½ oz. Cappelletti

½ oz. St. George Bruto Americano

Fresh grapefruit juice, to top

1. Place all of the ingredients, except for the grapefruit juice, in the rocks glass and add a giant ice cube. Top with grapefruit juice and stir.

2. Garnish with the grapefruit wheel and enjoy.

GLASSWARE: Collins glass
GARNISH: Pickled vegetables, Hogwash Mignonette (see recipe)

HOG ISLAND BLOODY MARY

A Bloody Mary is one of those cocktails that should be overly complicated—and with 12 different ingredients, this one certainly delivers. Despite the almost overwhelming number of flavors present in the drink, it comes together shockingly well. And the garnish of pickled vegetables adds a sour note that can be a welcome reprieve from the drink's peppery heat.

6 oz. vodka

12 oz. tomato juice

1 oz. seasoned rice vinegar

1 oz. unseasoned rice vinegar

1 oz. Worcestershire sauce

1 oz. fresh lemon juice

1 oz. extra-hot prepared horseradish

16 dashes Tapatio or Crystal hot sauce

8 dashes of celery bitters

4 pinches of salt

20 cracks of black pepper

1. Place all of the ingredients in a pitcher and whisk to combine.

2. Fill 4 glasses with ice and pour the drink into them.

3. Garnish with pickled vegetables and the Hogwash Mignonette and enjoy.

HOGWASH MIGNONETTE: Place 1 minced large shallot, 1 minced large jalapeño chile pepper, and ½ bunch of fresh cilantro, finely chopped, in a bowl and stir until well combined. Just before serving, stir in the juice of 1 lime, ¼ cup seasoned rice vinegar, and ¼ cup unseasoned rice vinegar and serve. Use all of the mignonette the same day it's made.

GLASSWARE: Coupe
GARNISH: Luxardo maraschino cherries

GREEN GOBLIN

If you like cocktails with an herbal flavor profile, you'll want to try the Green Goblin. With botanical vodka, basil, and Green Chartreuse among its ingredients, it's a drink that feels fresh, earthy, and absolutely packed with flavor.

8 fresh basil leaves

1 (heaping) teaspoon caster (superfine) sugar

1¼ oz. Square One Botanical Vodka

½ oz. Green Chartreuse

¼ oz. Maurin Quina

¾ oz. fresh lime juice

1. Chill the coupe in the freezer.

2. Place the fresh basil and sugar in a cocktail shaker and muddle.

3. Add ice and the remaining ingredients and shake until chilled.

4. Double-strain into the chilled coupe, garnish with Luxardo maraschino cherries, and enjoy.

GLASSWARE: Nick & Nora glass
GARNISH: 3 espresso beans

ESPRESSO MARTINI

With coffee culture continuing to thrive and a number of producers offering quality coffee liqueurs, the Espresso Martini has seen a major resurgence of late. This one includes both cold brew and Mr Black's exceptional coffee liqueur, and some condensed milk to balance out any bitterness with sweetness and richness.

¾ oz. vodka

1 oz. cold-brew coffee

1 oz. Mr Black Coffee Liqueur

¼ oz. sweetened condensed milk

1. Place all of the ingredients in a cocktail shaker, fill it two-thirds of the way with ice, and shake until chilled.

2. Double-strain into the Nick & Nora glass, garnish with the espresso beans, and enjoy.

GLASSWARE: Collins glass
GARNISH: Makrut lime leaf

THE NOMAD

Makrut-Infused Vodka. Coconut milk. Lavender bitters. Sparkling wine. Truly, the Nomad is a study in subtle flavors. This isn't a drink that will overpower you with flavor—it's one to sip slowly and appreciate every last drop.

2 oz. Makrut-Infused Vodka (see recipe)

½ oz. Simple Syrup (see page 40)

½ oz. fresh lime juice

1½ oz. unsweetened coconut milk

2 dashes of Scrappy's Lavender Bitters

1½ oz. JP Chenet Brut Sparkling Wine

1. Place all of the ingredients, except for the sparkling wine, in a cocktail shaker, fill it two-thirds of the way with ice, and shake until chilled.

2. Strain the cocktail into the Collins glass, add ice, and top with the sparkling wine.

3. Garnish with the makrut lime leaf and enjoy.

MAKRUT-INFUSED VODKA: Combine 10 grams makrut lime leaves with 1 liter of Townes Vodka. Let the mixture steep for 24 hours. Strain before using or storing.

GLASSWARE: Cocktail glass
GARNISH: Rose petal

GRAVE WATER

This morbidly named cocktail includes two different types of vodka, complemented by elderflower liqueur, rose water, and grapefruit juice. Garnished with a rose petal, the result is something equal parts floral and botanical. The aroma from this cocktail will draw you in, and its drinkability will show you that there's absolutely nothing to fear.

1 slice of cucumber

2 oz. Ketel One Vodka

1 oz. Ketel One Botanical Grapefruit and Rose Vodka

1 oz. St-Germain

½ oz. rose water

1 oz. fresh grapefruit juice

1. Place the cucumber in a cocktail shaker and muddle.

2. Add ice and the remaining ingredients and shake until chilled.

3. Double-strain into the cocktail glass, garnish with the rose petal, and enjoy.

GLASSWARE: Mason jar
GARNISH: Slice of watermelon

WATERMELON DAYS

The cocktail itself is little more than vodka and lime juice, but the addition of fresh watermelon (and a jalapeño slice for a little bit of kick!) make it an ideal summer sipper.

2 oz. Dripping Springs Vodka

4 watermelon cubes, finely chopped

1 slice of jalapeño chile pepper

½ oz. fresh lime juice

1. Place all of the ingredients in a cocktail shaker, fill it two-thirds of the way with ice, and shake vigorously until chilled.

2. Pour the contents of the shaker into the mason jar, garnish with a slice of watermelon, and enjoy.

GLASSWARE: Cocktail glass
GARNISH: Green cocktail cherry

SAPPORO

There isn't much to the Sapporo—it's almost the cocktail version of an amuse-bouche. But vodka, amaretto, Green Chartreuse, and dry vermouth are a potent combination of flavors. It will only take a couple sips to finish this cocktail, but you'll savor each one. Originally created in 1972 by famed Japanese bartender Tatsuro Yamazaki, the Sapporo has remained popular in Japan ever since.

1 oz. vodka

2 bar spoons amaretto

2 bar spoons Green Chartreuse

2 bar spoons dry vermouth

1. Place all of the ingredients in a mixing glass, fill it two-thirds of the way with ice, and stir until chilled.

2. Strain into the cocktail glass, garnish with the green cocktail cherry, and enjoy.

GLASSWARE: Cocktail glass
GARNISH: 1 strip of grilled yuzu peel

YUZU & MATCHA MARTINI

Yuzu? Matcha? They will be unfamiliar to many home mixologists, but they each add an unmistakable element to this delicious, colorful cocktail, which is sure to get you thinking about other ways you can make use of these two ingredients.

1½ oz. vodka

1 oz. fresh grapefruit juice

1 bar spoon yuzu juice

1 bar spoon matcha powder

1. Place all of the ingredients in a cocktail shaker, fill it two-thirds of the way with ice, and shake until chilled.

2. Strain into the cocktail glass, garnish with the strip of grilled yuzu peel, and enjoy.

GLASSWARE: Cocktail glass
GARNISH: Sudachi wheel, shell ginger leaf

APOTHECARY

Sudachi is a tart, green Japanese citrus fruit. Chances are, most American drinkers won't be familiar with it—and that's a shame, because it adds a wonderful green note to this twist on the classic Gimlet.

20 dried juniper berries

¼ shell ginger leaf

2 oz. vodka

⅔ oz. fresh sudachi juice

2 bar spoons Simple Syrup (see page 40)

1. Use a mortar and pestle to grind the juniper berries and shell ginger leaf into a fine powder.

2. Place the mixture in a cocktail shaker. Add the remaining ingredients and ice and shake vigorously until chilled.

3. Double-strain into the cocktail glass, garnish with the sudachi wheel and shell ginger leaf, and enjoy.

GLASSWARE: Rocks glass
GARNISH: Houjicha leaves

AMALFI TO OSAKA

I've included a handful of Negroni recipes in this book, and the reason for that is simple: it's my personal favorite cocktail and I'm always fascinated by a unique take on its classic recipe. The Amalfi to Osaka certainly is unique, eschewing gin for vodka and using a combination of half Campari, half Martini & Rossi Bitter to create something that still feels like a Negroni, but is undeniably its own thing.

⅔ oz. Houjicha Vodka (see recipe)

⅔ oz. Mancino Rosso Vermouth

2 bar spoons Campari, chilled

2 bar spoons Martini & Rossi Bitter, chilled

1. Place an ice sphere in the rocks glass and add the ingredients in the order they are listed in.

2. Stir, slowly, putting air in the drink without melting the ice.

3. Sprinkle houjicha leaves on top of the ice sphere. Use enough to give the drink a distinct aroma, but not so much that it slides into the drink.

   HOUJICHA VODKA: Add 15 grams of loose-leaf houjicha tea to 1 (750 ml) bottle of vodka and steep for 2 days. Strain before using or storing.

GLASSWARE: Cocktail glass
GARNISH: Green cocktail cherry

ETRENNE

Created by legendary Tokyo bartender Akihiro Sakoh, the Etrenne drinks like a combination of banana bread and mint chocolate chip ice cream. A lovely pale green in color, it's a rich and creamy cocktail with an unusual flavor profile. Banana and mint might not seem like a natural combination, but both can be excellent cocktail ingredients when used with a deft hand. Sakoh's hand is certainly a deft one, and the result here speaks for itself.

½ oz. vodka

⅔ oz. green banana liqueur

2 bar spoons mint liqueur

½ oz. heavy cream

1. Place all of the ingredients in a cocktail shaker, fill it two-thirds of the way with ice, and shake vigorously until chilled.

2. Double-strain into the cocktail glass, garnish with the green cocktail cherry, and enjoy.

WINE, LIQUEURS & OTHER SPIRITS

Throughout the history of making cocktails, liqueurs were little more than sidekicks, supporting players, there to help the principals look their best. They were invaluable, essential, but seen as not being versatile or deep enough to carry the weight for an entire cocktail. They were one-note, capable of being additive, but incapable of occupying a prominent place. But, as with a Neil Young guitar solo or Mariano Rivera's cutter, sometimes we discover that a pony with one trick, if it is deployed expertly, proves to be irresistible. There is something appealing about a cocktail that boldly leads with the effortless complexity of an amaro, the spicy, bitter citrus of Campari, or the vegetal, herbaceous, and tobacco flavors present in Green Chartreuse, a fearlessness that appeals to our minds and tests the tastebuds in unexpected and delightful ways.

One benefit of a drink built around liqueurs and other off-the-well-worn-path spirits is that they cause us to pause where we would otherwise breeze past, cause us to take a moment and appreciate some aspect that had always been hidden away, crowded out by some other element. In a way, they allow us to love what we love in a deeper, fuller manner. So, whatever your favorite occupant of the "second-tier" is, start thinking about ways to elevate it to the fore, and celebrate it in full.

GLASSWARE: Coupe
GARNISH: Plum Paint (see recipe)

CHERRY BLOSSOM

This is a high degree of difficulty cocktail that will prove extremely rewarding once you do pull it off. One tip: The Plum Paint should not break away from the glass when you strain the cocktail into it. If it does, the paint was made incorrectly. Instead, you want it to slowly leach into the glass as you sip, turning the cocktail a light pink as you consume it.

1¼ oz. shochu

¾ oz. Roku Japanese Gin

¼ oz. white crème de cacao

½ oz. Cherry Blossom Syrup (see recipe)

¾ oz. fresh lemon juice

1. Chill the coupe in the freezer.

2. Place all of the ingredients in a cocktail shaker, fill it two-thirds of the way with ice, and shake until chilled.

3. Brush the bowl of the chilled coupe with the Plum Paint, double-strain the cocktail into the coupe, and enjoy.

CHERRY BLOSSOM SYRUP: Place 200 grams cherry blossom paste, 500 grams sugar, and 500 grams water in a blender and puree until combined. Use immediately or store in the refrigerator.

PLUM PAINT: Place 100 grams dried plum powder and 10 oz. water in a blender and puree on high until smooth. Use immediately or store in the refrigerator for up to 1 week.

GLASSWARE: Footed pilsner glass
GARNISH: Lemon wheel, lime wheel, apple slices, fresh mint

PROPER CUP

If you're an Anglophile, mix a batch of this clever riff on the Pimm's Cup. The light touch of the Apple Syrup ties all of the flavors together, and the double dose of bitters provides plenty of depth.

2 cucumber ribbons

2 oz. Pimm's

¾ oz. Hendrick's Gin

Dash of Angostura Bitters

2 dashes of Peychaud's Bitters

½ oz. fresh lemon juice

½ oz. fresh lime juice

1 oz. Apple Syrup (see recipe)

Ginger beer, to top

1. Place the cucumber ribbons in the footed pilsner glass.

2. Place all of the remaining ingredients, except for the ginger beer, in a cocktail shaker, fill it two-thirds of the way with ice, and shake vigorously 20 times.

3. Strain into the glass and top with ginger beer.

4. Garnish with the lemon wheel, lime wheel, apple slices, and fresh mint and enjoy.

APPLE SYRUP: Slice an apple and place it in a medium saucepan with 1 cup water, 1 cup sugar, and ½ teaspoon pure vanilla extract. Bring to a boil over medium heat, reduce the heat to medium-low, and simmer for 5 minutes. Remove the pan from heat and let the syrup cool completely. Strain before using or storing.

GLASSWARE: Coupe
GARNISH: Spritz of mace tincture

MACE

In terms of aroma and flavor, Linie Aquavit is a powerhouse, making it a bit of a bull in a china shop when it comes to cocktails. But the earthiness of the beet juice, the richness of the syrup, and the bright flavor of Aperol keep it in line, resulting in this stylish serve.

|||||||||||||||||||||||||||||||||||||||||||||||||||||||||||||||||||||||||||||||||||||||||||||||||||||||||||||||||||||||||||||||||||||

1 oz. Linie Aquavit

1 oz. Aperol

½ oz. fresh orange juice

½ oz. freshly pressed beet juice

¾ oz. syrup from a can of Lucia young coconut

1. Place all of the ingredients in a cocktail shaker, fill it two-thirds of the way with ice, and shake vigorously until chilled.

2. Double-strain the cocktail into the coupe, spritz it with the mace tincture, and enjoy.

GLASSWARE: Collins glass
GARNISH: Shiso leaves

OMAR'S FIZZ

The Omar's Fizz is inspired by firnee, a popular Afghani custard dessert made with cardamom, pistachios, rose water, and saffron. Singani 63 is the national drink of Bolivia, and has only recently come to the attention of people outside the country. Distilled from grapes grown at a minimum of altitude 5,250 feet, it is sweet, tart, and possesses a seductive aroma.

1½ oz. Saffron-Infused Singani (see recipe)

1 oz. Vanilla Syrup (see page 81)

1 oz. fresh lemon juice

1 oz. heavy cream

3 dashes of cardamom bitters

1 egg white

Splash of club soda, to top

1. Place all of the ingredients, except for the club soda, in a cocktail shaker and dry shake for 10 seconds.

2. Add ice and shake until chilled. Let the cocktail rest for 30 seconds.

3. Strain over ice into the Collins glass and top with the club soda.

4. Garnish with shiso leaves and enjoy.

SAFFRON-INFUSED SINGANI: Place 2 pinches of saffron threads and a 750 ml bottle of Singani 63 in a large mason jar and let the mixture steep overnight. Strain before using or storing.

GLASSWARE: Coupe
GARNISH: None

NAKED & FAMOUS

The salmon pink color is a bit deceptive, as the drink is smoky thanks to the mezcal and bittersweet thanks to the Aperol. This mash-up of the Last Word and the Paper Plane was another massive hit from the folks at New York's Death & Co.

¾ oz. Yellow Chartreuse

¾ oz. mezcal

¾ oz. Aperol

¾ oz. fresh lime juice

1. Chill the coupe in the freezer.

2. Place all of the ingredients in a cocktail shaker, fill it two-thirds of the way with ice, and shake until chilled.

3. Strain into the chilled coupe and enjoy.

GLASSWARE: Cocktail glass
GARNISH: 14 drops of Angostura Bitters

DRINK OF LAUGHTER & FORGETTING

Take a trip through a book of classic cocktails and I'm betting you will be astounded by how many were born in New Orleans. While the Drink of Laughter & Forgetting is not as established as the Sazerac or Ramos Gin Fizz, it can stand shoulder to shoulder with any Crescent City product, thanks to the interplay between the Green Chartreuse and Cynar.

1½ oz. Cynar

½ oz. Green Chartreuse

¾ oz. fresh lime juice

½ oz. Demerara Syrup
(see page 20)

1. Place all of the ingredients in a cocktail shaker, fill it two-thirds of the way with ice, and shake until chilled.

2. Strain into the cocktail glass, garnish with the bitters, and enjoy.

GLASSWARE: Coupe
GARNISH: 7 drops of The Bitter Truth Cucumber Bitters

MAGIC TREE

Mastiha, a Greek liqueur made from the aromatic resin of the hyper-rare mastic tree, isn't an ingredient you're likely to find on a grocery store shelf. With a noticeable sweetness and notes of clove, however, it is one you'll find yourself returning to time and again after making this cocktail, which balances out the spirit's piney notes with a swish of lime and the cooling embrace of cucumber.

2 slices of cucumber

1½ oz. Stoupakis Homeric Chios Mastiha Liqueur

½ oz. Suze

½ oz. navy-strength gin (Royal Dock preferred)

¾ oz. fresh lime juice

¼ oz. Simple Syrup (see page 40)

1. Place the cucumber in a cocktail shaker and muddle.

2. Add ice and the remaining ingredients and shake until chilled.

3. Double-strain the cocktail into the coupe, garnish with the bitters, and enjoy.

GLASSWARE: Highball glass
GARNISH: Smoked paprika

JAPANESE WHISPERS

The primary ingredient in this cocktail is shochu, a Japanese distilled beverage commonly made from rice, barley, sweet potatoes, buckwheat, or brown sugar. Though sometimes compared to sake, shochu has a much stronger flavor—making it more akin to vodka than rice wine. Japanese Whispers is made from all Japanese ingredients, layering whisky and Passion Fruit Cordial atop its foundation. The addition of an egg white creates a lovely foam atop the drink, making it as visually arresting as it is flavorful.

|||||||||||||||||||||||||||||||||||||||||||||||||||||||||||||||||||||||||||||||||||||||||||||||||||||||||||||||||||||||

1⅜ oz. shochu

¾ oz. Suntory Toki Whisky

1 oz. Passion Fruit Cordial
(see recipe)

1 egg white

½ oz. fresh lime juice

½ oz. fresh lemon juice

1. Place all of the ingredients in a cocktail shaker containing no ice and dry shake for 15 seconds.

2. Fill the cocktail shaker two-thirds of the way with ice and shake vigorously until chilled.

3. Strain over ice into the highball glass, garnish with the paprika, and enjoy.

PASSION FRUIT CORDIAL: Place 17½ oz. passion fruit puree, 3½ oz. fructose, and 7 oz. caster (superfine) sugar in a mason jar and stir until the fructose and sugar have dissolved. Use immediately or store in the refrigerator.

GLASSWARE: Coupe
GARNISH: Lime wheel

MONTEZUMA

The Montezuma is a unique cocktail, with a boozy base of pisco, Midori, and Sauvignon Blanc blended with sweet, fruity kiwi puree. The result is an almost alarmingly green cocktail that foregrounds both melon and kiwi flavors. The inclusion of Sauvignon Blanc gives the drink an airy sweetness that complements the pisco perfectly—and how many cocktails call for an ingredient as interesting as kiwi puree?

1 oz. pisco

½ oz. Midori

1 oz. kiwi puree

1 oz. Sauvignon Blanc

¾ oz. Simple Syrup
(see page 40)

1. Place all of the ingredients in a cocktail shaker, fill it two-thirds of the way with ice, and shake until chilled.

2. Double-strain into the coupe, garnish with the lime wheel, and enjoy.

GLASSWARE: Brandy snifter
GARNISH: Orange twist

GO AHEAD ROMEO

There's something especially exciting about a drink whose character changes over time, and the Go Ahead Romeo is just such a concoction. Made with Prosecco and frozen Aperol ice cubes, the sweet, citrusy notes of the Aperol will make themselves increasingly known as the ice begins to melt, changing both the color and flavor of this delicious drink. It's a creative way to ensure that you get something different with each and every sip.

6 Aperol Ice Cubes
(see recipe)

4 oz. Prosecco

1. Place the Aperol Ice Cubes in the snifter and pour the Prosecco over them.

2. Garnish with the orange twist and enjoy.

   APEROL ICE CUBES: Combine ¼ cup Aperol and ¾ cup water, pour the mixture into ice cube trays, and freeze until solid.

GLASSWARE: Rocks glass
GARNISH: Fresh mint

DECI'S ROOMMATE

Made with a mix of rosé and brandy, this bright and bubbly cocktail is the perfect sipper for an early brunch or a hot summer afternoon. The mint garnish adds a nice aromatic element to the cocktail, preceding each sip with a cool, refreshing scent.

1 oz. Calvados

¾ oz. fresh lime juice

½ oz. Rich Simple Syrup (see page 48)

2 oz. sparkling rosé

1. Place the Calvados, lime juice, and syrup in a cocktail shaker, fill it two-thirds of the way with ice, and shake until chilled.

2. Add the sparking rosé to the shaker and strain over ice into the rocks glass.

3. Garnish with fresh mint and enjoy.

GLASSWARE: Collins glass
GARNISH: Lemon wheel, hibiscus blossoms, and Fabbri Amarena cherry

HIBISCUS TEA COBBLER

It's hard to imagine a more beautiful cocktail than the Hibiscus Tea Cobbler. Thanks to the hibiscus and grenadine, it projects an almost impossibly vibrant shade of red that permeates the entire glass. The cocktail itself is as flavorful as its coloration would imply, with the tart, floral notes of hibiscus playing well with the more muted tones of Cognac and curaçao. It's a cocktail that has a good deal more subtlety than its appearance might lead you to believe.

1 teaspoon grenadine

1 lemon wheel, sliced in half

1 oz. curaçao

1 oz. Cognac

1½ oz. Hibiscus Tea (see recipe)

1. Place the grenadine and lemon wheel in the Collins glass and muddle.

2. Add the remaining ingredients and then fill the glass with crushed ice.

3. Stir until the cocktail is chilled and combined.

4. Top the cocktail with more crushed ice, garnish with the lemon wheel, flowers, and cherry, and enjoy.

   HIBISCUS TEA: Pour 4¼ cups boiling water over 3½ oz. dried hibiscus blossoms and steep for 10 minutes. Strain the tea through cheesecloth and let it cool completely before using or storing.

GLASSWARE: Goblet
GARNISH: None

MOLE YETI

Tequila and stout beer go together extremely well, and the Mole Yeti augments that classic combination with the inclusion of chipotle powder and an herbal liqueur to create a cocktail that mimics the flavor profile of a classic mole sauce. It's rich, dark, and strong, with a welcome bit of heat from the chipotle powder. The velvety smoothness of the Mole Yeti makes it an ideal dessert cocktail.

1 oz. añejo tequila

¾ oz. Leopold Bros. Three Pins Alpine Herbal Liqueur

½ teaspoon chipotle chile powder

6 oz. chocolate stout

1. Place the tequila and liqueur in a mixing glass, fill it two-thirds of the way with ice, and stir until chilled.

2. Strain into a clean mixing glass, add the chipotle chile powder, and stir vigorously to completely incorporate it.

3. Strain into the goblet, slowly pour in the stout, and enjoy.

GLASSWARE: Snifter
GARNISH: None

CHARTREUSE SLUSHY

Green Chartreuse is a spirit made from around 130 herbs and plants macerated in a sugar beet–based alcohol. It's a great complement to the tartness of lemonade in this sugary cocktail, helping to ground the sweet and sour flavors and create something eminently drinkable.

‖‖

2¼ oz. tart lemonade

1 oz. Green Chartreuse

2½ oz. Rich Simple Syrup
(see page 48)

1. Place all of the ingredients in a blender, add 4 oz. crushed ice, and puree until smooth.

2. Pour the drink into the snifter and enjoy.

GLASSWARE: Snifter
GARNISH: Lime wheels, freshly grated cinnamon

CARRIED AWAY

Made with a base of aquavit and coconut liqueur, Carried Away is an interesting mix of flavors. The addition of fresh lemon juice and Honey Syrup bring just a little something extra to this cocktail, pushing it over the top to create something truly great.

1½ oz. Krogstad Aquavit

¾ oz. Rhum Clément
Mahina Coconut Liqueur

½ oz. fresh lemon juice

¼ oz. Honey Syrup
(see page 35)

1. Place all of the ingredients in a cocktail shaker, fill it two-thirds of the way with ice, and shake until chilled.

2. Strain over ice into the snifter, garnish with the lime wheels and cinnamon, and enjoy.

GLASSWARE: Collins glass
GARNISH: None

REJECT IN THE ATTIC

Dismissing Jägermeister as being solely for college students is selling your-self, and the spirit, short. In truth, its herbal, almost medicinal quality makes it a perfect foundation for a wide range of cocktails, as the Reject in the Attic shows.

1 oz. Jägermeister

1 oz. Amaro Lucano

¾ oz. Cocchi Americano

¼ oz. Clear Creek Logan Berry Liqueur

Q Grapefruit Soda, to top

1. Fill the Collins glass with ice and build the cocktail in the glass, adding the ingredients in the order they are listed.

2. Gently stir and enjoy.

GLASSWARE: Rocks glass
GARNISH: 2 to 3 dashes of Scrappy's Lime Bitters

SAKE NIGHT IN CANADA

Pierre Ferrand Dry Curaçao is a personal favorite of mine—if you're looking to elevate your home bar, it's a great place to start.

2 oz. sake

½ oz. Singani 63

¼ oz. Pierre Ferrand Dry Curaçao

1 oz. aquafaba

¾ oz. grapefruit juice

¼ oz. Rich Simple Syrup (see page 48)

1. Place all of the ingredients in a cocktail shaker, fill it two-thirds of the way with ice, and shake until chilled.

2. Strain over ice into the rocks glass, garnish with the bitters, and enjoy.

GLASSWARE: Coupe
GARNISH: Lemon twist

CHAMPS-ÉLYSÉES

A simple drink, without any particularly fancy liqueurs—just high-quality ingredients working in perfect harmony with one another.

2 oz. VSOP Cognac

¾ oz. fresh lemon juice

¼ oz. Green Chartreuse

¼ oz. Simple Syrup
(see page 40)

2 dashes of Angostura
Bitters

1. Place all of the ingredients in a cocktail shaker, fill it two-thirds of the way with ice, and shake until chilled.

2. Double-strain into the coupe, garnish with the lemon twist, and enjoy.

GLASSWARE: Wineglass
GARNISH: None

IN THE DAY WE GO ON FOREVER

Pommeau is a French spirit made by mixing apple juice with apple brandy, and it makes the perfect complement to Prosecco in this fresh and fizzy cocktail. The drink takes its name from Jeannette Winterson's novel *The Passion*, set during the Napoleonic Wars, but you'll find no conflict in this glass—just artfully blended flavors and the perfect amount of bubbles with every sip.

2 oz. Prosecco

1½ oz. LeMorton Pommeau

½ oz. Amaro Montenegro

¼ oz. fresh lemon juice

1 oz. club soda

¼ oz. Passion Fruit Syrup (see page 48)

1. Place 5 ice cubes in the wineglass, add all of the ingredients, stir until chilled, and enjoy.

GLASSWARE: Collins glass
GARNISH: Fresh mint

GREEN GODDESS PUNCH

If you've never had absinthe, this recipe is a perfect entry point. Despite its reputation, absinthe does not, in fact, cause hallucinations nor insanity. In reality, it's just a liqueur with a licorice-like flavor that goes nicely with a little lime juice and simple syrup. Green Goddess Punch is a straightforward cocktail that highlights the flavor of the absinthe without too many distractions.

½ oz. absinthe

1 oz. fresh lime juice

1 oz. Simple Syrup
(see page 40)

4 oz. Topo Chico

1. Fill the Collins glass with ice and build the cocktail in the glass, adding the ingredients in the order they are listed.

2. Gently stir, garnish with fresh mint, and enjoy.

GLASSWARE: Tiki mug
GARNISH: Orange slice, Luxardo maraschino cherry

CAMPARI COLADA

As its name suggests, the Campari Colada is essentially a Piña Colada made with Campari instead of rum. If that sounds odd to you, well, join the club. But it turns out the bitter, herbal notes of the Campari blend perfectly with the pineapple juice and coconut cream. Top it with whipped cream, and this is a perfect after-dinner cocktail.

3 oz. fresh pineapple juice

1 oz. cream of coconut

1 oz. heavy cream

2 oz. Campari

1. Place all of the ingredients in a cocktail shaker with no ice and dry shake for 10 seconds.

2. Fill the tiki mug with crushed ice, pour the cocktail over it, and then use the swizzle method to mix the drink: place a swizzle stick between your hands, lower the swizzle stick into the drink, and quickly rub your palms together to rotate the stick as you move it up and down in the drink. When frost begins to form on the outside of the tiki mug, the drink is ready.

3. Garnish the cocktail with the orange slice and maraschino cherry and enjoy.

GLASSWARE: Collins glass
GARNISH: Strip of orange peel

TUMUGI

There are two unique elements to this cocktail: tumugi and yogurt liqueur. Tumugi is a spirit that is synonymous with Japan in the same way vodka is synonymous with Russia or rum is synonymous with Cuba. You won't find it in too many places in the US, but you should definitely give it a try if you see it. Yogurt liqueur is also unusual, and adds a slightly tangy sweetness to this cocktail to create a flavor profile like nothing you've ever tasted.

⅔ oz. Tumugi

½ oz. yogurt liqueur

Sweet ginger ale, to top

1. Place 2 large ice cubes in the Collins glass.

2. Add the Tumugi, then the liqueur, and top with ginger ale. Jiggle the mixture with a bar spoon to combine, garnish with the strip of orange peel, and enjoy.

GLASSWARE: Cocktail glass
GARNISH: None

L.I.T.

The L.I.T. cocktail is a simple, sake-based spin on a Cosmopolitan. Short for Lost in Translation, the L.I.T. was created by Japanese bartender Yasukazu Yokota with the goal of evoking the same sweet-sour balance as the movie. I'd have to say it worked—the addition of peach liqueur gives it some added sweetness without becoming cloying, and it plays well against the lime. Sake is a wonderful foundation for this drink, offering its own unique flavor that never overpowers.

1⅓ oz. sake

⅔ oz. cranberry juice

2 bar spoons peach liqueur

2 bar spoons cherry blossom liqueur

2 bar spoons fresh lime juice

1. Place all of the ingredients in a cocktail shaker, fill it two-thirds of the way with ice, and shake until chilled.

2. Strain into the cocktail glass and enjoy.

GLASSWARE: Rocks glass
GARNISH: Strip of orange peel

NEGRONI SBAGLIATO

All right—one last spin on a Negroni. Who needs gin when you can opt for effervescent Prosecco? Its bubbles really change the way this cocktail drinks, in a way that is unfamiliar but not entirely unwelcome. The flavor of the bitter Campari stands out even more against the sweet Prosecco, lending it an assertiveness that isn't always present in a classic Negroni.

1 oz. Campari

1 oz. sweet vermouth

Prosecco, chilled, to top

1. Place a large ice cube in the rocks glass, add the Campari and sweet vermouth, and stir until chilled.

2. Top with Prosecco, express the orange peel over the cocktail, garnish the drink with it, and enjoy.

GLASSWARE: Champagne flute
GARNISH: Orange twist

RITZ COCKTAIL

Cognac, orange, and maraschino topped with chilled Champagne—that's a combination capable of making anyone feel fancy. The Ritz Cocktail manages to be both elegant and playful at once, taking classic flavor combinations and punching them up with a bit of fizz. It's sweet, citrusy, and absolutely delicious.

¾ oz. Cognac

½ oz. curaçao

¼ oz. Luxardo maraschino liqueur

¼ oz. fresh lemon juice

Champagne, chilled, to top

1. Chill the Champagne flute in the freezer.

2. Place the Cognac, curaçao, and Luxardo in a mixing glass, fill it two-thirds of the way with ice, and stir until chilled.

3. Strain into the chilled Champagne flute and top with Champagne.

4. Garnish with the orange twist and enjoy.

GLASSWARE: Wineglass
GARNISH: None

ELDERFLOWER SPRITZ

I've always been partial to elderflower in cocktails, so I simply had to get this unorthodox serve from Colleen Jeffers in this collection. A garnish of rosemary and a grapefruit twist are the only additions to this simple drink, releasing a bittersweet, herbal aroma with every sip.

||||||||||||||||||||||||||||||||||||||||||||||||||||||||||||||||||||||||||||||||||||||||||||||||||||||||||||||||||||||||||||||

1 sprig of fresh rosemary

1 strip of grapefruit peel

1½ oz. elderflower liqueur, chilled

Prosecco, chilled, to top

1. Chill the wineglass in the freezer.

2. Rub the rosemary and strip of grapefruit peel around the inside of the wineglass and set them aside.

3. Pour the liqueur into the glass and top with the Prosecco.

4. Gently add ice to the cocktail, place the rosemary and strip of grapefruit peel on top, and enjoy.

GLASSWARE: Champagne flutes
GARNISH: Slices of pear, fresh rosemary

SPICED PEAR PUNCH

Sparkling wines are great for making crowd-pleaser cocktails, and the Spiced Pear Punch is a perfect example. The comforting flavor combination of cinnamon, lemon, and pear forms a solid foundation for this cocktail, while the bubbles from the Champagne make it supremely drinkable. Sure, you could just add a bottle of Champagne to some fruit punch at your next party. Or you could elevate the drinking experience with something truly memorable. The ingredients below should provide you with 16 servings.

3 cinnamon sticks

1 cup 100 percent pear juice (not from concentrate)

1 cup sugar

2 cups Krogstad Aquavit, chilled

2 cups amontillado sherry, chilled

1 cup fresh lemon juice

1 (750 ml) bottle of Champagne, chilled

1. Crush the cinnamon sticks and place them in a medium saucepan. Add the pear juice and sugar and bring to a boil, stirring to dissolve the sugar.

2. Reduce the heat, cover the pan, and simmer for 5 minutes. Remove the pan from heat, keep the cover on it, and let the syrup steep overnight.

3. Strain the syrup through a fine-mesh sieve into a punch bowl. Add ice and the aquavit, sherry, and lemon juice and stir until chilled.

4. Gently top the punch with the Champagne, garnish the punch with slices of pear and fresh rosemary, and enjoy.

WEIGHTS

1 oz. = 28 grams
2 oz. = 57 grams
4 oz. (¼ lb.) = 113 grams
8 oz. (½ lb.) = 227 grams
16 oz. (1 lb.) = 454 grams

VOLUME MEASURES

⅛ teaspoon = 0.6 ml
¼ teaspoon = 1.23 ml
½ teaspoon = 2.5 ml
1 teaspoon = 5 ml
1 tablespoon (3 teaspoons) = ½ fluid oz. = 15 ml
2 tablespoons = 1 fluid oz. = 29.5 ml
¼ cup (4 tablespoons) = 2 fluid oz. = 59 ml
⅓ cup (5⅓ tablespoons) = 2.7 fluid oz. = 80 ml
½ cup (8 tablespoons) = 4 fluid oz. = 120 ml
⅔ cup (10⅔ tablespoons) = 5.4 fluid oz. = 160 ml
¾ cup (12 tablespoons) = 6 fluid oz. = 180 ml
1 cup (16 tablespoons) = 8 fluid oz. = 240 ml

TEMPERATURE EQUIVALENTS

°F	°C	Gas Mark
225	110	¼
250	130	½
275	140	1
300	150	2
325	170	3
350	180	4
375	190	5
400	200	6
425	220	7
450	230	8
475	240	9
500	250	10

LENGTH MEASURES

1/16 inch = 1.6 mm
⅛ inch = 3 mm
¼ inch = 6.35 mm
½ inch = 1.25 cm
¾ inch = 2 cm
1 inch = 2.5 cm

INDEX

ABOUT CIDER MILL PRESS
BOOK PUBLISHERS

Good ideas ripen with time. From seed to harvest, Cider Mill Press
brings fine reading, information, and entertainment together between
the covers of its creatively crafted books. Our Cider Mill bears fruit twice
a year, publishing a new crop of titles each spring and fall.

"Where Good Books Are Ready for Press"

501 Nelson Place
Nashville, Tennessee 37214

cidermillpress.com